The P
Bauge

Judy Cuddeford

J.b.Cuddeford

Mount Publications

ISBN 1 900571 08 2

Published by
Mount Publications, PO Box 1916,
Chelmsford, Essex, CM3 1EY,
England.
www.mountpub.com

Prelude

It was an autumn night, cold and dark with a damp white fog hovering over the fields. There was no moon, and no lights could be seen from the village. The only sounds to be heard were the footsteps and heavy breathing of two men as they made their way slowly along the lane. One of them struggled to carry a large heavy sack over his shoulder and the other carried two spades. The first man, the older of the two, was thickset and stocky in comparison to the other, a tall gangly youth. The second man tripped and swore loudly as he stumbled, causing his companion to turn clumsily and hiss at him to be quiet. They passed the churchyard, where the grave markers loomed eerily through the fog, and turned down another lane towards a copse of trees beyond the village. On reaching the edge of the wood the first man grunted as he dropped his heavy load from his shoulder and sat down on a tree stump to catch his breath. He turned to his companion and whispered to him to go and find a suitable place. The second man put the spades down and crept off into the trees, returning a few moments later to tell his companion that he had found what they were looking for. The first man heaved his burden back on his shoulder, and followed the other deep into the copse. On reaching their chosen spot he again lowered the sack to the ground, and then each took up a spade and proceeded to dig. Even though it was a cold night the two men were soon sweating and panting from their exertions. They stopped and glanced warily around, their ears straining for a warning of anyone's approach, but all remained still. They removed their cloaks and resumed digging, their rasped breath visible in the cold night air. All that could be heard was the muffled sound of the spades as they dug. At last he decided that the hole was deep enough, and he motioned to his companion to stop digging. Together they took up the burden, and slithering on the damp grass they hauled the sack down into the hole. Scrambling out, they paused to regain their composure, nerves taut and eyes straining in the gloom. Certain that they were still alone, they swiftly backfilled the hole, covering it with leaves and broken branches until no trace of their activities could be seen. Hoisting the spades back onto their shoulders they returned to the village as silently as they had left it. As they reached the village the older one stopped, took hold of the younger ones arm and turned to speak to him.

'You must never tell anyone what we have just done tonight. It must be our secret, and we must carry the knowledge of it with us to our graves.' With that the father put his arm around his son's shoulder and together they walked down the lane to their home and the welcoming warmth of the fire.

Chapter 1

It was one of those spring days when everything seems right in the world and nothing could possibly go wrong. The sun was shining, the hedgerows were full of primroses and cowslips, the hawthorn was in blossom and the air smelt fresh and clean. Rissa stepped into her blue hatchback car and set off down the gravelled driveway humming along to the radio which she had on at nearly full volume-she was happy. She was soon to marry her fiancé Simon Middleton, their house was nearly completed and she had a loving family. The only blot that she could see on her near perfect life was that Richard Harvey their local vicar had disappeared the week before Easter. He was supposed to preside at her wedding in just over two week's time but she was sure he would turn up and the mystery would be explained.

Richard, a tall, quite good looking man in his mid-thirties, had arranged to go to the diocese retreat house in a neighbouring village for a weekend of prayer and meditation with some of the local ladies from the bible study group. He left the village late on the Friday evening two weeks ago but had failed to turn up at the Retreat House and nobody knew where he was. Still, Rissa thought as she sped down the lane towards the village, he was bound to turn up.

Clarissa Montague (or Rissa for short) was the eldest daughter of Tom Montague, a prominent local landowner and farmer. Her mother had died when she was very small and her grandmother helped to bring her up until Tom had married her stepmother Sarah 11 years ago. Rissa lived at Chadsbury Hall, the rambling old house that had been in the family for generations. She shared her home with her father, stepmother and stepbrother and sister, Harry and Lucy aged 10 and 6 respectively. Her grandmother had moved out of the great house when Sarah came to live there and bought a small cottage in the village.

Rissa was very happy with her family; Sarah had always been like an elder sister to her and had been there during her teenage years to help her with all the problems that being a teenager entailed - clothes, boys and school. Her father was a kind man, hardworking and serious. Although he adored his daughter and would do anything for her he had found it difficult to cope with an emotional highly spirited teenager and was grateful for his young wife to help out with Rissa's more difficult years. Sarah an attractive brunette in her early thirties was a very capable mother and homemaker and she had made the family home come alive with laughter for Rissa and her two young siblings. Rissa was now 22 years old and since finishing at business college had worked in her fathers livery stables where she helped with the care of the horses (her grand passion) and managed the accounts of the business. Her father was a generous employer to his daughter and she was allowed plenty of time to oversee the building of her new home and the planning of her wedding.

She was at this moment on her way to visit the new house, that her father was building for her as a wedding present. The house was being built on some land that her family owned at the edge of the village. It was positioned on a slight rise overlooking the village with a small stream running through what would be the bottom of the garden. The house itself was nearly completed and the decorators were busy putting the finishing touches to it. She knew she was very lucky to have such a house to start her married life in. As you entered the front door there was a large farmhouse kitchen to the right running from the front to the back of the house and to the left a lounge of similar size to the kitchen also running from the front of the house to the back. In between the kitchen and lounge at the back of the house was the dining room and off the hallway were a small cloakroom and the stairs up to the first floor. Above the kitchen was a large airy master bedroom with dressing room and en-suite bathroom and there were a further two bedrooms and a family bathroom. A small flight of stairs led up from the landing into the loft, which had been made into a large room running the whole length of the house. This they intended to use as a study, but it could be converted into a playroom or further bedroom at a later date. The views to the rear of the house were stunning and when the gardens were completed the house would be magnificent. Simon's parents, not to be outdone by Tom Montague, were paying for the gardens to be landscaped as their wedding present. This was the reason for Rissa's early morning visit; she intended to discuss the work with the landscape gardener. As she turned into what would be the driveway of 'Brook House,' their new home, she saw Jake Allen waiting to meet her and almost jumping up and down with excitement.

Jake Allen was 19 years old, well over six feet in height, slim with tanned arms and legs and curly blonde hair. An only son with six sisters, he had struggled at school where he had been cruelly taunted for his difficulties with reading and writing. Despite this he had a sunny disposition and a wonderful smile, and had most of the local girls swooning at his feet. He came from a local family who had lived and worked in the village for generations. His father owned a small building firm, and it was they who had done most of the work on the house. Having left school at sixteen, Jake now worked as a labourer for his father, and was at this moment helping to lay a patio. He worked hard, and was always eager to help the elderly in the village. His pride and joy was his motorbike, and most of his spare time was spent either riding or cleaning it.

Rissa slowed the car to halt as he came running over to the driver's door, and as she opened the door he spoke saying,

'Quick Rissa, you've got to come - we've found a body!'

Chapter 2

Rissa stepped out of the car; she was a tall well-built girl with long golden brown hair and a freckled complexion. Her hair today was neatly tied in one long French plait and she was dressed in a white tee shirt, blue jeans, a navy-blue blazer and brown leather loafers.

She bent down, removed the keys from the ignition and picked up her battered brown leather rucksack and then turned to the youth standing by the car impatiently hopping from one foot to the other.

'What do you mean you've found a body?' Her immediate thoughts turning to the disappearance of Richard Harvey.

'Oh, it must be old, it's only a load of old bones, but you must come and see, Rissa, they are round the back by the house where we are laying the new patio.' Jake turned from the car and proceeded to walk towards the house. Rissa slammed the car door shut, locked it and followed him.

Although the interior of the house was nearly completed the outside still looked like a building site with various tools and rubble lying about, a skip and an assortment of vehicles including a brand new silver BMW.

'That must belong to Charles Forsyth the landscape gardener,' Rissa thought, 'obviously his business must be doing well.'

She picked her way round the debris and followed Jake around the side of the house to find a number of people crouching or peering at something on the ground outside the lounge. She recognised all of them. There was Jake's father, George Allen, Bert and Fred his two workmen, the two painters and to one side the slightly effete figure of Charles Forsyth. Charles was a small man who spoke in an affected way but Rissa knew that looks can be deceiving and that he was a very astute business man, happily married with three young children.

As Jake and Rissa turned the corner of the house the group of men all stopped what they were doing and turned to look at Rissa. George spoke first.

'I suppose that young Jake has told you what we've found. It looks like it has been here for a long time but we thought it best not to touch it and we were just about to contact the police.'

Charles, who had his mobile telephone in his hand, turned to Rissa and asked,

'I don't suppose you have the number of the police in Kilborough, do you darling?'

Rissa shook her head and approached the men, crouched down on the ground and looked to see what they had unearthed.

All she could see was some bones and what looked like a human skull covered in dirt. The men had obviously stopped digging when they realised what they had found. She could see that there were still bones sticking out of the earth and also what appeared to be a coin, but it was very heavily encrusted and she wasn't sure. Still crouching she turned to Charles and suggested he contacted Directory Enquiries for the telephone number of the police. He nodded and wondered why he hadn't thought of that himself. He obtained the telephone number and called the local police station and asked to speak to the sergeant on duty. Rissa could hear only one side of the conversation and Charles appeared to be answering a lot of questions, he then finished on the phone, turned it off and turned to tell everyone what had transpired.

'Well, I've spoken to the sergeant on duty and he said that as we thought the bones were old he would contact the local coroner's office and the local archaeological unit. A policeman and someone from the archaeology unit would be over here before lunch. He also said that we weren't to touch the bones and that he didn't want us to talk about it to anyone until after they had visited and that he would like all of us here when they came.'

It was only just after nine a.m. and so George suggested that Bert put the kettle on and they all had a cup of tea. The painters could then get back to work and the rest of them could continue working on the patio at the other end from the bones.

Rissa suggested that after the tea she and Charles should go over the plans for the rest of the garden.

The gardens when they were finished were intended to be almost maintenance free, for although Rissa and Simon would enjoy pottering in the garden, they didn't intend to spend all their time maintaining it as they had plenty of other things to do. Both of them were keen outdoor types and Rissa spent most of her free time riding, but she also enjoyed going for long walks and on her holidays was a keen skier and water skier. Simon too enjoyed skiing but he spent most of his spare time out on his mountain bike or when he got the chance rock climbing with friends in Wales or Scotland.

The patio was to run the whole length of the house, with sliding glass doors leading from both the lounge and dining room and a further door from the kitchen. Simon had said when he had first seen the house design that the house was a window cleaner's dream come true and he hoped Rissa wasn't going to expect him to clean all the insides of the windows. The patio would be surrounded by a small wall and from the centre there would be steps leading down to a lawn which would roll down to the brook at the end of the property's boundary. On the left-hand side Charles had suggested a small rockery and one or two larger beds for flowers and in front of the kitchen a small herb garden and vegetable plot were planned. It was intended to plant an orchard in the field next to the house. To the front of the house there was going to be a paved drive sweeping round to a double garage and small workshop. They would put the rest of the front to lawn, with just two flower borders on the side of the drive.

Charles had laid out the plans on the dining room floor and he and Rissa studied them with Rissa commenting on the plants he had chosen and making a few suggestions herself. The morning seemed to disappear and when they heard a car pulling into the front Rissa was surprised that her watch said that it was 11.30 a.m.

She went out through the front door to meet the new arrivals. They were a uniformed police sergeant and a tiny young woman with short cropped mousy brown hair. She was wearing a huge faded blue sweatshirt which reached almost to her knees, and her legs were encased in faded blue jeans with holes in them. On her feet she wore a pair of trainers that had seen better days and on her nose were perched an enormous pair of spectacles which hid most of her face. They reached the front door and the policeman introduced themselves.

'Good morning, I am Sergeant Bridges of the Kilborough police and this is Miss James from the county archaeological unit. We had a call from here

14

about some bones and have come to investigate them. Perhaps you could tell me who you are?'

Rissa explained who she was and made the introductions as by now everyone else had gathered behind her.

'Hello Joe,' said George. 'How's the dart playing then?' Apparently George knew the sergeant quite well, as he played for a rival darts team from a pub in the next village. George was captain of the village darts team, which played at the Angel pub - a very successful team which had won the local brewery championship for the last five years.

'Oh, hello George, I might have guessed it would be you digging up bodies. I hope we've finally caught you in the act and that you are one of those mass murderer types,' said the sergeant laughingly.

'I think I would have been very young to start if this is one of mine,' George retorted.

Rissa gestured to the sergeant and Miss James to enter through the front door and they all trooped through the house and out of the dining room to the patio. Rissa pointed at the bones and the sergeant and Miss James moved over to look at them. Miss James knelt on the ground and peered closely at them through her huge glasses. She turned to the sergeant and asked if it was all right if she picked the skull up. Sergeant Bridges had taken one look at the bones and decided it wasn't a job for the police, so he nodded his head. Miss James picked up the skull and studied it closely, and then she picked up the coin and turned it over in her hands. She then looked up to Rissa.

'Hi, my name is Anne, I'm with the County Archaeological Unit but I am based at the County Museum in Kilborough. I would hazard a guess and say that these bones are certainly very old. I believe this coin to be a medieval half-groat of the 15th century, which would put these bones at a similar age, but we would need to excavate the skeleton and look for any other evidence before reaching a conclusion. However we will need to obtain an exhumation order before we can proceed further.'

Sergeant Bridges nodded in agreement and suggested that she contact them to see if they could authorise it quickly, as he didn't want the bother of organising a guard over these old bones until they were allowed to remove them.

Anne took her mobile phone from her pocket and rang the County Archaeologist. She asked him to contact the Coroner and request an exhumation order, and to let her know the outcome. She then turned to the others and said that they would now have to wait. By this time Bert was grumbling that it was about time for their dinner break. George agreed that they might as well knock off. Sergeant Bridges interjected and asked them to eat their sandwiches on site. Until the bones were exhumed and safe he didn't want the whole village turning up to gawk.

There was a sound of a mobile phone bleeping causing all those present with one to check if it was theirs. It turned out to be Rissa's, and she removed it from her rucksack and answered it – it was Simon.

'Hi, Simon, I'm still at the house,' she said. 'Yes, I realise I have been here a long time but something has come up which will take too long to explain. I'll meet you in the Angel tonight.'

Just as she finished there was the sound of another phone bleeping and this time it was Anne's. She answered it and had a lengthy conversation, after which she turned to the others with a large smile on her face.

'That was the county archaeologist; the coroner is happy with our assessment of the situation here and he has obtained an exhumation order which will be issued today. My boss says that I can continue to excavate the site and report to him with my findings.'

Sergeant Bridges breathed a sigh of relief; he was not going to have to call a police constable over after all. He spoke to Anne.

'Miss James, I will leave you here then and trust you will report the outcome of your findings and let me know if the police will be required further.

As I brought you here how will you get back to town?' Rissa interrupted and said that she would be happy to run Anne back to town when she had finished.

The policeman left and the workforce went and ate their lunch. Charles said that if he wasn't needed he would be off. Anne asked him not to speak to anyone about the discovery until that evening, and Rissa said she would give him a call later but he said not to bother, as he would pop into the Angel.

The two girls were left alone on the patio and Rissa asked Anne if she wanted some lunch. It was agreed that Rissa would drive down to the Angel and buy some sandwiches and something to drink for their lunch, and she promised not to say anything in the pub.

Rissa got into the car and drove down to the village; she was really quite excited by the morning's events and wondered to herself who the remains belonged to.

On returning to the house Rissa found Anne on her knees by the skeleton, carefully scraping away with a small trowel. Rissa suggested that Anne stopped work and the two girls sat on the dining room floor and ate their lunch. Rissa had bought two large French bread rolls filled with tuna and salad, with two bags of crisps and cans of cola. Rissa laid the food out on the floor and they munched on the sandwiches and drunk from their cans saying little. When they had finished they continued to sit for a while and talked to each other asking questions and getting to know one another. There was an instant rapport between the two of them and both of them liked each other instantly although they seemed so dissimilar. Rissa the tall well built, well groomed wealthy country girl and Anne the small, dark rather scruffily dressed scholar.

Rissa told Anne a little about herself and explained about her wedding and how the house was been built for them by her father as a wedding present. Anne said that she had only been in Kilborough for two months, and that she was originally from Manchester. She said how she found the sleepy southern town very different. She was currently living in a rented flat overlooking the marketplace and enjoying her job but so far she had made few friends. Rissa suggested that she came down to the Angel in the village that evening to meet Simon, and she was sure there would be some nice eligible young men there. Anne agreed and asked coyly if Jake was taken or did he have any older brothers. Rissa laughed and said she would see what could be found.

Rissa also asked Anne about her job and said that she found it all fascinating and could she stay to help? Anne agreed and they picked up the remains of their picnic, dropped it in the skip and returned to the skeleton. Anne suggested that as she removed the bones Rissa cleaned each one with a brush which she removed from her bag. They could hear the painters' radio blaring out from the house and Bert and Fred were busy at the other end of the patio with Jake happily doing all the more mundane tasks such as removing the rubble and earth to the skip. Every so often he stopped and came over to the girls to see what they were doing, extracting promises from them that he would be the first to know if anything really exciting was found.

As Anne was carefully removing the bones from the ground she suddenly stopped, asked Rissa for the brush and then painstakingly began to clear earth away from something she had found. Rissa leant over her shoulder to see what it was. It appeared to be some sort of badge or brooch. Although there was some corrosion the piece was in remarkable condition and seemed to be in the shape of a scallop shell. Anne was quite excited and told Rissa that the scallop shell was generally attributed to pilgrims in medieval times and that she would be able to clean this one up so as they might ascertain its origin. Anne delved into her bag and produced a plastic envelope into which she placed the badge and the coin previously found. They then continued with their task. Anne found two more coins that she also placed in finds bags and just when she had decided she had retrieved all the bones she spotted one further artefact which appeared to be a silver cross, although it was heavily discoloured. When Anne was convinced there was nothing more to be found they decided to call it a day. As they had promised they called Jake over and showed him what they had found. He was very impressed and Rissa asked him if he would like to join them for a drink that evening. He blushed and said that he would and went back to his work.

Anne asked Rissa what she wanted to do with the bones as they belonged to her. Rissa was surprised and said that she would like to see them assembled as a whole skeleton. Rissa also said that she would like to help Anne try and find out who it was, to which Anne agreed. Rissa went into the house and returned with a cardboard box that had contained some of the kitchen units. They placed the bones in the box, and then set off for the museum in Kilborough with the box in boot of Rissa's car. As it was nearly 5 p.m. Rissa dropped Anne off at the museum and agreed to see her that evening before setting off for home.

Chapter 3

Rissa drove home through the village and turned in through the wrought iron gates of Chadsbury Hall. The long drive tree-lined drive led to a large court-yard in front of the house. The house had no particular style as over the centuries it had been knocked down, rebuilt and added onto. Today the main part of the Hall consisted of a Queen Anne style house with Victorian additions added on the side. Rissa parked her car at the front of the house grabbed her bag, bounding up the front steps to be met at the door by Lucy her 6 year old sister and Boris and Teddy, the family's black labrador and golden retriever. There was a great deal of tail wagging and tongue licking on the part of the dogs. Lucy gave Rissa a large grin, said she would see her later and ran down the steps with the dogs at her heels. Lucy was a cute child with Rissa's colouring and her hair was is in its usual style of two long plaits. She was a solitary child who was never happier than when she was messing around with the dogs in the garden or riding her beloved pony, Bubbles. Today as usual she was dressed in jeans, anorak and trainers. She was going to be a brides-maid at Rissa's wedding and was very excited about it and the dress she would be wearing.

Rissa entered the front door and turned towards the small sitting room where Sarah her stepmother could often be found at that time. As she reached the door of the sitting room she heard raised voices from inside and identified them to be her father and Sarah. She opened the door and entered the room. The two occupants turned as she entered and stopped speaking. Her father normally a quiet reserved man was standing by the window his face red and angry. Sarah who was normally calm and serene was also flushed.

'What's the matter?' asked Rissa.

'Ask her!' replied her father pointing his finger at Sarah and with that he strode quickly to the door, brushed pass Rissa and left the room. Rissa turned to Sarah who by this time was breathing normally.

'Oh it's nothing for you to worry about, just your father and I having a disagreement, I'll make it up to him while we are getting ready to go out this evening,' said Sarah, dismissing the subject. 'Sit by me and tell me about your day.'

Rissa related the day's event to her stepmother who was very interested, and said that she was sure Rissa's father would be too. Rissa reminded Sarah that she was taking Lucy into Kilborough for a dress fitting the next day and would she like her to take Harry to be fitted for his morning suit. She could then take them to the museum with her and also out for lunch. Sarah nodded, remarking that it was a good idea and that Rissa might have more success taking Harry than she would, especially if there was a treat involved. She also asked if they could get together and check that all the wedding arrangements were on schedule. They agreed to meet at home for afternoon tea.

Rissa and Simon were to get married the last week of April in the local church and Sarah had offered to arrange the reception. In this she was in her element. She was a very successful organiser of events, and before her marriage she had attended catering school and then worked for a large firm of caterers in the city of London.

The reception was to be held in a large marquee on the lawn at the rear of the house. There was going to be a sit-down meal for family and close friends and in the evening a buffet supper and dance for all their other friends and the villagers. Rissa knew that it would be a great success and agreed to see Sarah for afternoon tea the next day.

As Sarah and her father were going out to dine with friends that evening, Rissa said that she had better go and find the housekeeper to tell her she would be eating tea with the children. She stood up and left the room, frowning and wondering what on earth she had stumbled across earlier. She went down the hall to the kitchens to find Mrs White, the housekeeper-cum-cook.

After speaking to Mrs White she knocked on the door of her father's study. He told her to wait a minute and she then heard him unlock the door and open it. When he saw who it was he smiled weakly and turned back to sit at his desk. Rissa was concerned his eyes were red and bloodshot as though he had been crying. She knew better than to say anything and instead perched on the end of his desk and told him all about the body they had found and her interest in the mystery surrounding it. Her father asked her some searching questions and said that he would help her if he could. He was very interested in the history of the village and the family, both were mentioned in the Domesday Book and he said he would try and find his copy for her and any other documents that may be of interest. Clarissa kissed her father on the cheek and left him to his musings in search of her tea.

Rissa entered the large homely kitchen to find Mrs White just putting the kettle on. There was a tantalising aroma of food cooking which, Rissa was told, was a Lancashire hotpot just ready to be taken out of the oven.

Mrs White had been with the family since Sarah married Rissa's father. She was a homely middle aged woman who ran the household ably under the supervision of Sarah and with the help of two women who came to clean from the village. She was a competent cook and complemented Sarah very well whose own cooking tended to be more exotic than Mrs White's. The two women worked very well together and Mrs White never resented her young mistress's visits or interference in the kitchen.

Rissa carried the teapot through into the small dining room adjacent to the kitchen. This was the room where the family ate most of their meals unless they were entertaining. It was a large sunny room with views over the lawns at the back of the house. The formal dining room was located at the front of the house and was rather dark and cold on sunless days, with its high ceilings. As Rissa sat down, the door from the hall crashed open and Harry raced in followed by Lucy and the dogs. Mrs White came in from the kitchen bearing a casserole, saw them and sent them out again to wash their hands. They returned moments later after a very quick wash. They sat down and Mrs White placed the casserole dish in front of Rissa and left them to it, knowing that Rissa was more than capable of controlling her siblings.

'I've heard about the skeleton - it's gruesome!' said Harry excitedly. 'Can we come and see it?'

Rissa was always amazed at how fast news travelled in the village but then she remembered whom Harry would have been with all day. Harry was a typical 10-year-old; skinny with golden brown hair like Rissa's which although well cut always managed to look like it was never combed. Like all boys of his age he was mad about football and played at the weekends in the five-a-side league. As it was still the

Easter holidays he had spent the day with his partners in crime, the Allen twins. The two youngest Allen girls were ten-year-old twins, Nicola and Sophie. They should have been born boys as they were very good football players and spent most of their free time with Harry either playing football or getting into trouble around the village.

'I suppose Jake told you,' Rissa replied and proceeded for the third time that day to tell her tale. She then reminded Lucy that they were going for a dress fitting the next morning and that she had discussed it with their mother and if Harry promised to behave, he could come too and they would visit the museum to look at the skeleton. She would then take them both to the local burger bar for lunch. She also said there was a catch as it would be an ideal opportunity for Harry to be fitted for his Morning Suit as the dress hire place was next door to the dressmakers.

Harry looked at her in horror but then agreed, as viewing the skeleton was too good an opportunity to miss. He had flatly refused to be a pageboy at the wedding but was secretly pleased that they had asked him to be an usher and guide the guests to their seats in the church, and he was taking the role very seriously.

They finished the hotpot and the two younger ones had vanilla ice cream to finish with. They then cleared the dirty plates through into the kitchen to be loaded into the dishwasher and raced off upstairs to their sitting room to watch television. Rissa helped Mrs White load the dishwasher, wash up and lay the table for breakfast, and then she too went upstairs to her bedroom.

Her bedroom, like her brother's and sister's, was on the second floor. It consisted of a bedroom, sitting room and bathroom. It was one of the first things Sarah had done when she had come to Chadsbury Hall, to convert these rooms into a suite for Rissa and help her decorate it. It was one of the many things that she had done for Rissa that had helped Rissa to love her. The suite was at one end of the house; the bedroom at the front and quite dark, but the sitting room/study had windows to the side and the back of the house and was light and airy. Rissa sat at the window looking out over the gardens, pondering over the events of the day. She was worried about her parents, but at the same time excited about the possibility of discovering the identity of the skeleton.

She stood up and went into the bathroom to have a shower and wash her hair. She dried her hair and tied it back in a ponytail. She then dressed in a wine-coloured silk shirt, tight black velvet jeans and black riding boots. As it was a nice evening she decided to walk to the Angel and so she sprayed herself with Dolce Vita, slipped on an old trench coat, picked up her rucksack and left for the pub.

As she walked down the stairs, she met her parents just leaving their bedroom holding hands and smiling. They've obviously made up thought Rissa to herself grinning. They were dressed to go out for dinner at friends in a nearby village. Her father was dressed in smart green wool jacket with tan trousers and sported a brightly coloured tie. Sarah, elegant as usual was dressed in a short black dress and jacket and high heels, her only adornment a string of pearls around her neck. Rissa said she hoped they enjoyed themselves and left to walk to the village.

Chapter 4

Rissa arrived at the Angel just after 8 p.m. The church clock had sounded just as she entered the village. She had enjoyed her walk down to the village; it was about a mile from the Hall and at that time of the evening the lanes were quiet. She had passed the end of the lane that led to Brook House and wondered if she and Simon would call in on their way home, she hoped so. There was plenty to show Simon since he had last been there but she was also thinking that they would able to be alone together, indeed she had left a blanket and some cushions up there for that very purpose a few weeks ago. Recently their time alone together had been less than she would have liked, with both of them so busy with work, their new house and planning the wedding. Still, it wouldn't be long before she would have him all day every day for two whole weeks when they went for their honeymoon. They were going to spend two weeks in the Caribbean; one week would be spent in Antigua where they would spend their days water skiing, snorkelling and swimming. As for the nights Rissa was sure they would take care of themselves! The second week they were going to cruise amongst the smaller islands on a full-masted sailing ship.

The Angel pub was on the other side of the road to the church and at the end of the village green. It was a large rambling thatched timber framed building, the sort of pub that epitomised rural England. In fact the whole village gave the impression that it had stepped out of the pages of a book on the English countryside. A road ran through the village and on one side was the church and an assortment of houses whilst on the other was the village green. The Angel overlooked the green and on the other side from the road was an unpaved road and further houses. The village hall sat next to the church and behind this was the cricket pitch and children's play area, with a football pitch at the bottom end of the village. The village no longer had a shop; it had closed a few years ago when Miss Little had retired. Dora Little had had the shop converted into a house and she now lived there with Edith, also a spinster and a retired schoolteacher. These two sisters were like chalk and cheese, Dora was a plump cheery woman but Edith was thin and gaunt with never very much to say unless it was to criticise.

Rissa entered the Angel lounge bar and was immediately greeted by John Mallory, the landlord.

'I hear you have a visitor at your new house; I wouldn't fancy being there on my own late at night.'

'Take no notice of him,' his wife Dawn interrupted.

John and Dawn Mallory had taken on the pub 5 years ago. They came from the north of England where he used to work down the mines. They had fitted into the village life easily and were well liked. Dawn was an excellent cook and John knew how to keep a good pint. The pub was a lively place most nights and there were also plenty of activities including a very good darts team and the occasional quiz night or theme night. It was very much a village pub but on a summer's evening the gardens would be full of visitors out for a drive and a good meal.

Rissa ordered a white wine spritzer and turned from the bar to survey the room. She saw a number of people she knew from the village. Dezi Shah was standing at the corner of the bar with a pint of lager in front of him talking to Julian Talbot-Simpson and she nodded hello. She liked Julian and his wife but found Dezi Shah very difficult although she felt sorry for his wife. 'I must go and visit her next week,' she thought.

Dezi Shah and his wife had lived in the village for less than a year and they did not really belong. Dezi ran a wholesale grocer on the outskirts of Kilborough and he joined in all the activities of the village, was a good cricketer but he was still considered to be an outsider. His wife in contrast found it difficult to join in; she was very unhappy living in the village and longed to return to live in Leicester among her relatives and friends.

The Talbot-Simpsons, Julian and Fiona, also had

just moved to the village. They were a typical 'yuppie' family with high-powered jobs in the city and a nanny to look after their two young children. They had made no deliberate effort to be part of the village but they had managed to do just that. Their children attended the playgroup at the Village Hall, Fiona baked cakes for the local bazaars and Julian played the organ in the church.

She saw Simon sitting with Jake and his sister Jenny at a table in the corner by the fire and she went over to join them.

Jenny, another of Jake's sisters, was seventeen years old and since she had left school had worked for Rissa at the livery stables. She shared Jake's good looks with the same curly blonde hair and hazel eyes. Besides Jenny and the twins, Jake had three older sisters; Julie and Joanna were both married and Jane lived away from home training to be a nurse.

Jake stood up and moved round so that Rissa could sit on the seat next to Simon.

'You're not cleaning your bike or playing darts tonight then?' said Rissa to Jake.

'He told me all about the skeleton that you found, and persuaded me to come with him here to hear all about it,' interrupted Jenny. Jake sat quietly nursing his pint of bitter but his eyes kept wandering to the door of the pub each time it opened. 'He seems very taken with the lady archaeologist that visited today,' she said laughingly digging him in the ribs. Jake spluttered into his beer and blushed. Jenny and Jake were good friends as well as being brother and sister and it was Jenny and Jane who helped protect him from the cruel taunts of the other children at school.

Simon put his arms around Rissa, gave her a big hug and nuzzled her ear.

'You smell good,' he whispered, and then in a louder voice. 'They've been filling me in on all the days' events and said that you and the young archaeologist would tell me more when you came.'

Dawn Mallory then called to Simon from the bar to say that his food was ready. He went to the bar to collect it, returning with a steaming bowl of Dawn's chilli-con-carne with fresh white crusty bread, which he placed on the table. He explained to Rissa that he hadn't eaten that day, as there had been a problem for him to sort out at the factory.

Simon had studied engineering and management at university and since he completed his degree he had worked for his father. His father owned a small engineering firm in Kilsborough that specialised in high precision parts for the aircraft industry. Simon was the engineering manager but his father was gradually giving him more responsibility so that he could semi-retire and spend more time on the golf course.

As Simon ate his meal, Rissa spotted Charles

Forsyth sitting in the corner with his pretty young wife. They were both just finishing a meal and Rissa went over to them and told them about what Anne had found. She suggested they joined her group but Charles said that no they had to get back to the children. She returned to Simon and the others and as they discussed the days events, Jake's parents, George and Eileen, came in through the door and stopped at their table before collecting their drinks and going through into the bar and the dart board.

Eileen like her husband was a good darts player. She was a busy woman who had brought up her seven children and still found time to run the local WI, be in charge of the church flower rota and play darts.

'George told me about the goings on today,' she said. 'What with that and the Vicar's disappearance we seem to have plenty in the village to talk about.' Rissa asked her if she had any further news about Richard Harvey. 'No, but I was talking to your grandmother this morning while we doing the church flowers and she said that his sister had arrived at the Vicarage and had been asking questions. Your grandmother said that the police had been notified and they would be questioning all the ladies from the bible study class tomorrow. That means your grandmother and I as well as the Misses Little. Mind you, I hope it's the police that do the questioning and not that awful sister of his.'

Susan Harvey, Richards's sister had only visited her brother in the village on a few occasions and each time she had managed to irritate the ladies of the village. She was unmarried, in her early forties and had spent her time criticising her brother, his church and the local community.

George took hold of his wife's arm and steered her in the direction of the dart board, he knew that once she had started talking she would never stop and he wanted them to practise their darts for next weeks match.

As Simon finished his meal the door to the pub opened and Anne entered, her petite figure encased in black leathers and carrying a motorbike helmet. At the sight of her Jake grinned, stood up and rushed over to meet her.

'I didn't know you rode a bike, what is it?' he asked.

'Oh yes I've' been mad about bikes for years, I have a supersports 600 that I bought when I got this job.'

Jake asked her what she would like to drink and bought it and they both joined the others by the fire. It was obvious that Jake was smitten by Anne but she too seemed to be taken by the young Adonis. When Jake left them to go the gents, Jenny turned to Anne and said. 'You be careful with my brother, I don't want him getting hurt.' Rissa and Simon laughed, as the thought of the tiny Anne hurting Jake seemed incongruous, but Anne smiled and told Jenny not to worry.

The evening passed quickly and as last orders were called the group all stood up to go. Jenny to her bed, Jake and Anne to look at Anne's bike and Simon and Rissa to Simon's car.

The cold air hit them as they left the warmth of the pub and Rissa shivered as Simon led her to his car. His car, the other love in his life he once said jokingly to Rissa, was a sports car that his father had bought him for his 25th birthday.

'Shall we go and inspect the house,' Rissa said as she shut the door of the car. 'There is plenty to show you,' Simon turned to her and squeezed her knee.

'I know what I want you to show me,' he replied. He drove out of the car park and headed towards Brooke House, he parked the car at the front door and they both got out.

'Do you want to see where the skeleton was found?' asked Rissa

His answer was to turn her towards him and give her a long sensuous kiss. 'I'd rather be inside,' he said, as his hands moved between their bodies inside her coat to rub against her breasts beneath the silken blouse. As his hands started to explore lower Rissa gave a small moan in the back of her throat and she broke free and went to open the front door. There was electricity connected but they didn't turn on the light; instead they found their way up the stairs by the moonlight to the main bedroom. The decorating of this room was complete but there were no curtains and the moon gave them enough light to see each other by. Rissa collected the cushions and blanket from the cupboard where she had put them and placed them on the floor. She removed her coat and took hold of Simon and proceeded to undo the buttons of his shirt covering his chest with light feathery kisses. Her hands clutched his buttocks and she pulled him closer and rubbed herself against him. She then undid his trousers pulled down his boxer shorts and held him in her hand; he groaned. She then knelt on the floor and took him in her mouth. Simon took hold of her hair, releasing it from its band so that it dropped freely about her. He then pulled her to her feet, released her, and removed his clothes.

He was just under six-foot tall with a muscular body from all his athletic activities. It was smooth with only the lightest of hair covering his chest. Rissa too removed her clothes, throwing them in a heap in the corner. When they were both totally naked they stood looking at each other in the moonlight and then Simon moved towards Rissa lifting her off her feet and kissing her on the mouth. They stumbled and fell together on to the cushions on the floor and it was Simon's turn to discover the delights of Rissa's body. He stroked her breasts with his fingers and sucked at her nipples. His hands moved down her body stroking as they went until he reached the entrance between her legs which was moist and beckoning. Unable to wait any longer he turned her onto her back and entered her in one strong stroke; he then stopped, enjoying the feel of her engulfing him before continuing with rhythmic thrusts which got faster and faster. Rissa met every thrust with her own, her head writhing from side to side until they were both on the brink. With a loud grunt Simon climaxed just as Rissa's eyes opened wide and she too grunted with pleasure. They then both became still; Simon kissed her on the lips and whispered.

'Thank you.' He then rolled off her and reached for the blanket with which he covered them both, their arms still wrapped around one another.

Chapter 5

The next morning Rissa rose to another day of spring sunshine. She stepped into the shower singing to herself and thinking of the night before when Simon and she had made love. She was looking forward to when they were married and she could spend all night in his arms. Simon had returned her to Chadsbury Hall in the early hours of the morning. The house was in darkness and she quietly let herself in and went to bed.

She dressed quickly in a dark grey suit and white blouse and went down to breakfast. The rest of the family was already seated at the table eating their breakfast. Her father as usual was reading the paper at the same time as eating his toast and marmalade. Sarah sat at the other end of the table enjoying a light breakfast of a grapefruit and coffee. The two children were eating cornflakes and drinking orange juice. Rissa poured herself a cup of coffee and helped herself to muesli from the sideboard.

'We didn't hear you come in last night,' muttered her father from behind his paper.

'No, I don't suppose you did,' replied his daughter. 'It was late when we left the pub and we called in at Brook House on the way back.' She exchanged glances with Sarah and grinned. 'Eileen Allen was saying in the pub that the police are going to question grandma and the other bible study ladies about the vicar's disappearance today.'

Her father put his paper down and looked at his wife.

'Well that will be interesting, anyway I must be off.' He turned to his two younger children, gave them some money for sweets, told them to behave, stood up and left the room saying that he would see them all later.

Rissa looked at Sarah; she thought her father was behaving very oddly whenever the vicar was mentioned. Sarah said nothing but continued to eat her grapefruit. Harry and Lucy asked to leave the table and were told not to get dirty and to be in the hall in half an hour. They left the room, the dogs following at their heels. They were both dressed very differently to their usual attire. Lucy was wearing a short tartan kilt with a green jumper and matching tights with her hair like Rissa's in one long French plait down her back. Harry too looked almost tidy in smart black jeans, a check shirt and V-necked pullover.

'As you can see I managed to have them dressed respectably this morning,' said their mother. 'I too must be off as I am meeting the caterers this morning. I'll see you at 4pm.' She also left the room.

Rissa finished her breakfast thinking about the strained atmosphere there seemed to be this morning. She then cleared the pots through into the kitchen for Mrs White and went to collect her rucksack and car keys.

When she returned downstairs she found Harry and Lucy waiting for her. Lucy had put on her old anorak and Rissa sent her off to change in to a smarter coat. Harry was wearing his Barbour that met with Rissa's approval. When Lucy returned wearing her new smart blue jacket they shouted goodbye to Mrs White and left the house. Rissa allowed Harry to sit in the front but said his sister was to sit in the front on her return. Just as they set off their father came out and they all waved.

As they drove towards Kilborough Rissa thought that although she had been allowed plenty of time off in the weeks leading up to the wedding she must visit the livery stables after lunch to put some hours in on the accounts.

On arriving in Kilborough Rissa parked the car in the marketplace and they set off for the dressmakers, calling in the newsagents on the way to purchase sweets with the money their father had given them. They first went into the dressmakers where Mrs Danby, the dressmaker greeted them. Rissa left Lucy in Mrs Danby's capable hands and she and Harry went next door to the dress hire shop. The staff were very accommodating and it took them no time at all to sort out what Harry would require. They assured her that she could leave him alone with them while he was being measured and Harry promised to come next door when he was finished. Rissa returned to the dress-maker.

She opened the door to find Lucy standing patiently in the middle of the floor chattering away to Mrs Danby who was on her knees pinning up the hem of Lucy's dress. She looked every inch a bridesmaid. The dress was in pale green silk with short puffed sleeves, dark green smocking on the bodice with a full skirt of ballerina length. There was a wide dark green velvet sash tied around Lucy's waist and on her feet were dark green satin ballerina pumps.

'You look great,' Rissa exclaimed to Lucy. She then asked Mrs Danby if Fay had been in for her fitting. Mrs Danby said that she had called in last night and her dress was nearly complete.

Rissa was only going to have two bridesmaids, Lucy and Simon's sister Fay. Lucy was going to walk in front of the bride carrying a basket of flowers and Fay was to follow behind the bride. Fay was 18 years old and was working in the local vets for a year before going off to university to study to be a vet herself. Fay was tall, slim and pretty and she was one of those people who seemed to float through life without a care in the world. She was very clever with a great sense of humour and she and Rissa were good friends. Her dress was to be in the same green silk as Lucy's but it was to be a straight figure hugging sheath with shoestring straps and a green velvet bolero.

When Mrs Danby had finished with Lucy she dressed in her own clothes and Mrs Danby sat her in a corner with a glass of orange squash and a comic and then went to get Rissa's dress. The dress was made of white muslin. The top had a low neckline with long tight sleeves, and flowed out from beneath the bust in a style of the heroines in Jane Austen novels. Rissa tried it on and it fitted her perfectly. The bodice was beautifully embroidered and a white satin sash pushed her breasts up high showing off her freckled cleavage. It reached to her ankles and she was to wear white satin embroidered slippers.

Mrs Danby made some small adjustments and jokingly told Rissa not to put any weight on. The door to the shop opened and in walked Harry who stood there and whistled in admiration at his sister. He too was given a drink while Rissa changed into her street clothes. They then thanked Mrs Danby and left the shop to walk to the museum.

It was short walk to the museum and when they reached it they went into the entrance hall and asked for Anne. While they waited they all looked at the display cases in the hall. Rissa had not been there for years but Harry had been on a school trip recently and was telling Lucy all about the things on display. Anne came down the stairs to greet them.

Today she was not looking as scruffy as the day before. She was wearing a long peasant style skirt with a baggy jumper and on her feet were a pair of patent laced boots. She greeted Rissa and was introduced to Harry and Lucy. They were both asking her questions about the skeleton and if they could see it. Anne said that they would all go and look at it and then Harry and Lucy could look around the museum while she and Rissa talked. She led the way down a passage and through a door marked private into a large room with a table in the centre. On the table were the bones of the skeleton, assembled as they would have been in a body. She told the children not to touch and they all went to the table to look at the skeleton. It was about the same height as Rissa and Anne said that all of the bones were there and she had asked an expert on bones to come and look at it to see if they could learn more about it.

Harry and Lucy were very impressed and seemed at a loss for words. When they had all spent some time studying it Anne suggested they went and looked at the rest of the museum under the watchful eye of one of the museum assistants. Anne then led Rissa upstairs to her office.

'You and Jake certainly seemed to hit it off last night,' said Rissa. 'I hope you took note of what Jenny said, if you lead him astray you will have the whole of the Allen clan breathing down you neck.'

All of this was said lightly and Anne took it as such.

'Oh, I realise he's younger than me and not quite my intellectual equal but you have to admit he is good looking,' replied Anne. 'I also happen to like him, he's good company and a bike enthusiast like me. Tomorrow we are going to go out for a ride together and then who knows.'

'Well I hope you enjoy yourselves and I'm not so sure Jenny's right it may be you who has to take care,' said Rissa

'Anyway, enough about my future love life,' said Anne. 'I have some far more interesting things to show you.'

They had by then reached Anne's office and they both went inside. The room was small and apart from a desk and two chairs was crammed full with books and files.

'I have been studying that badge we found and comparing it to some in a book on medieval pilgrims' badges.' Anne picked up the badge from the desk and showed it to Rissa. 'I've cleaned it and as you can see it is made of pewter and the bottom part is a scallop shell and the upper part is the body of a man. Comparing it pictures of others I have seen I am nearly sure that it is the upper part of the body of St James. That is to say St James of Compostella. This could mean that the owner of this badge has been on a pilgrimage to Santiago de Compostella in Northwest Spain. Saint James was a popular figure with pilgrims so it may not be that this one had visited Spain but it would be nice to think so.'

Rissa was fascinated and asked if she could hold the badge, and as she took it from Anne's hands she felt as if she was that pilgrim.

Francis hurried through the village towards the house by the church where he was staying with his uncle. Henry Wodewarde was the parish priest in the small Essex village of Chadsbury Green. He was getting on in his years and welcomed his young nephews help.

Francis was 25 years old and until then had spent most of his life at a monastery in Northern England training to be a monk. At the completion of his training last year he had gone with two other monks from his monastery on a pilgrimage to Spain. For the young monk who had spent most of his life in the cloisters this journey had been quite an adventure and not all of it pleasant. They had suffered a great deal of hardship and on the way one of his companions had fallen ill and died before reaching Santiago de Compostella. The other two had completed their pilgrimage and returned to England. Francis felt in the pocket of his habit for the badge of St James, which he had collected in Spain.

His colleague had returned to the north but it

had been agreed that Francis was to spend a year helping his uncle. He was to help with the day to day running of the church and he also hoped to do some teaching of the villagers while he was there. Francis was a scholar and had spent many years at his monastery reading and writing and he was master of both Latin and French. He was a quiet studious young man and would have been considered good looking if it was not for his dull brown monks' habit and tonsured hair. He had been sent away to be monk before he was 10 years old and it was considered a great honour for his family. He had left behind his parents and six brothers and sisters who had been allowed to visit him once a year. He found over the years that he had grown apart from his family, finding little in common with them but Henry, his father's elder brother, was well educated and Francis enjoyed sitting with him in the evenings talking about literature and travel. The past year had opened his eyes and Francis was not sure if he would be satisfied spending the rest of his days in the monastery. He also was unsure about the life his uncle led as he found it difficult to communicate with the people who lived in the village. These were his thoughts as he hurried home to Henry.

Anne was still talking about the badge and Rissa reluctantly handed it back.

'We still have to find out how the pilgrim died, but maybe the 'expert' will be able to help us,' Anne continued. 'I also have been digging around in the local records and came across quite a lot of information about Chadsbury Green and the Hall. Some of it is quite old and written in Latin or old English but a local historian translated a lot of it earlier this century. I have some copies for you to take home if you like.' Rissa nodded and took the box file that Anne handed to her saying that she had better collect Harry and Lucy as she had promised to take them to the burger bar. They exchanged telephone numbers and agreed to meet soon, with that Rissa left Anne's office collected her charges and they set off for the burger restaurant.

Chapter 6

Rissa was quiet on the way back home; not that it mattered as her two companions talked incessantly about their outing to Kilborough. Rissa dropped them off at the Hall and then drove to the livery stable where she spent the next two hours in the office making sure the accounts were up to date. As she was leaving to meet Sarah for tea, she saw Jenny in the yard and they talked for a while about matters relating to the stable. Neither of them mentioned Jake and Anne.

Rissa returned home and joined Sarah in the small sitting room. Sarah had just carried in a tray laid out with a pot of tea and some toasted teacake. Sarah said that Lucy and Harry had told her their version of the morning's events, but the dress fitting wasn't included. She would be interested to hear how the fittings had gone. Rissa reported that everything seemed to have gone smoothly but Harry would need some suitable shoes to wear. Sarah agreed and said that she had planned to take them both shopping in one of the larger towns on Monday before they returned to school on Tuesday. The conversation then turned to the rest of the wedding plans. Rissa had left most of these to Sarah who enjoyed the challenge and she seemed to have everything organised. Sarah showed Rissa the menu that she had now confirmed with the caterers. The wedding breakfast was to be three courses. The starter was to be fresh asparagus followed by a main course of roast rack of lamb with a minty hollandaise sauce. The desserts were to be a choice of profiteroles with hot chocolate sauce or summer pudding. Rissa approved of Sarah's choice and also thought the variety of dishes to be offered at the evening buffet would be ample.

Sarah didn't envisage any problems with the marquee and the tent erectors were also going to provide some luxury 'port-a-loos.' Rissa asked Sarah if she had discussed the flowers with Rissa's grandmother. Sarah said that she had and that they had agreed that Mary was to organise the church flowers with the help of Eileen Allen and that she was to be in charge of the arrangements in the marquee.

Rissa wondered aloud what she could do, to which Sarah jokingly replied.

'Make sure you turn up on the day.'

Rissa's thoughts then turned to the disappearance of Richard Harvey and she said to her stepmother,

'I am going to granny's for supper this evening and so I should find out how the questioning by the police went. Unless you have already heard?'

Sarah visibly shuddered.

'No, but I hope he comes back soon as it is causing no end of problems.'

'What do you mean?' asked Rissa.

'It's very complicated but I promise to explain soon,' said Sarah. 'Anyway what are your plans for the weekend?'

'Simon is going away with friends climbing this weekend; he reckoned it would be his last chance to escape for awhile. Tomorrow I am catching the early train up to London with Fay and we are going to shop for clothes for my honeymoon. I have no plans for Sunday.' explained Rissa. 'Was there anything you wanted from London?'

Sarah couldn't think of anything and so they finished their tea and went their separate ways.

Rissa went upstairs to her room collecting the file Anne had given her from the car on her way. She put the file on her desk and thought that after visiting her grandmother she would spend the evening examining its contents. She considered changing but decided her grandmother would approve of her outfit. As it was nearly six-o clock she went back down stairs and drove to her grandmothers.

Mary Montague lived in a small cottage overlooking the green. It had originally been two houses but her son had had them converted into one for his mother when she moved out of the Hall. When Rissa slowed to a halt outside her grandmothers, Dora Little was walking down the garden path. When she saw Rissa she hurried towards the car and before Rissa had opened the door started talking at her.

'We've had such excitement today my dear, that nice sergeant came to see us with a detective from Kilborough. My sister and I were asked a lot of questions about the young Reverend Harvey and they were very interested to hear about our bible study class and our weekend retreat. They said that Miss Harvey thought there were suspicious circumstances surrounding his disappearance. But I think he's probably gone away with a nice young lady and was too shy to tell anyone. He's such a quiet man. We tried to be helpful but I had gone into Kilborough on that day and hadn't seen him. Edith as usual was very quiet but she did talk to the detective on her own while I was showing my garden to the sergeant. Not that she told me what she said.' At this point Dora paused for breath. 'I've just been calling on your grandmother to see what she had had to say to them. She said you were coming to visit. It is nice when the young take time to visit us old folks.'

Rissa smiled at the chattering friendly elderly lady who she remembered with affection from when Dora ran the village shop. She had always been one to talk but never said an unkind word about anyone, which was more than can be said for her sister.

'I'm sure granny will tell me all about it Miss

Little, it was nice to see you and looking so well.' Rissa locked the car door and hurried up to her grandmother's door before Dora Little could carry on talking. Her grandmother opened her front door just as Rissa reached it.

'I see Dora caught you. I've been trying to ease her out of my door for the last quarter of an hour. She does go on so,' said Mary.

Rissa laughingly replied.

'I know what you mean. Anyway how are you granny?' And she bent towards the older woman and kissed her on the cheek. Mary said that she was fine and opened the door wider; Rissa entered into the tiny hall that always smelt of beeswax. Today she could also smell something delicious wafting in from the kitchen. Rissa followed her grandmother into the kitchen and Mary said that the meal was nearly ready and so would Rissa help her to carry it through to eat. Mary had laid a table for two in the glassed- in porch that ran along the back of the house. This room was where Mary spent most of the daylight hours and it was kept warm not only by the sun but also by central heating. From this room Mary was able to enjoy her small but well kept garden which at this time was a riot of colour from all the Spring flowers in the flowerbeds. Rissa asked about the visit from the police but her grandmother said that she would tell her all about it later.

They carried the dishes through and they sat

down and ate the meal that Mary had prepared. They enjoyed homemade fishcakes with a lemon and parsley sauce, served with new potatoes and spinach. A rhubarb crumble followed this. As they ate their meal they talked about the skeleton that had been found and also the mornings visit to the dressmaker. Rissa also told her grandmother about Anne James the historian and how she felt she had made a new friend. When the meal was finished Rissa sat back in her chair and declared, 'that was great granny but if I carry on like this I won't fit into my dress.' Mary laughed and suggested that they did the washing up and then they could sit down and have a chat. With the washing up quickly completed they took cups of tea through into the cosy sitting room and Mary related to Rissa the visit by the police.

'It was Sergeant Bridges that lives in High Wood and a young detective that came to visit me. They explained that Susan Harvey had contacted them, as she was concerned that she had had no contact with her brother for two weeks. They already knew he had disappeared as we had already contacted them when he didn't turn up at the retreat but at that time they said there was nothing they could do. Now two weeks had past they decided they had better make some enquiries and they were currently checking up with all his known acquaintances outside the area. They wanted to know from me everything about the day he went missing and also anything else I could tell them. I told them that I had spent the morning at the church, with Eileen Allen, doing the flowers and while I was there Richard had come into the church. He said he was looking forward to our weekend away and had planned a number of topics for us to discuss. He also reminded us to take some stout walking shoes as he intended to take us on a long walk. I pointed out that he had to remember that some of us were not as young as he was. When I left the church I went up to the Hall and had lunch with your father and Sarah. Your father left soon after lunch and I came home about mid afternoon. I pottered in the garden and then sat in my chair before going upstairs to pack. George Allen picked me up about 6pm and took Eileen and I to the Retreat House. When I arrived at the Retreat House we were shown to our rooms and then we went down to the communal dining room where we met Dora and Edith Little and the other ladies in our party. We ate a very nice supper and it must have been 8pm when we began to wonder where the vicar was. I asked the retreat warden but he said he had had no word from him and he then went and tried to phone the Vicarage. There was no answer. He told us there was probably no cause for alarm and something had probably cropped up. He suggested we all went to bed and he was sure Richard would be there next morning.

I woke up early on the Saturday morning and went downstairs to make myself a cup of tea. I looked outside but could see no sign of the vicar's car. When the others came down to breakfast we asked the warden to check again and as there was still no reply form the vicarage he contacted the police who said that there had been no accidents reported. We were all very worried and could see no point to staying on retreat so we all returned home to find the rest of the village as perplexed as we were.' Mary paused. 'The police then asked me of my impressions of Richard Harvey. I told them that he had only been in the village for two years but he was a very popular vicar. I said that I found him to be a very quiet man and although he was very friendly with the older ladies he seemed to be very shy around women of his own age or younger. I told them that I had never seen him with a lady friend or even a man friend.'

At this Rissa spluttered into her tea.

'Granny!'

'I do know these things happen,' continued Mary, 'not that it would go down too well in this village. I omitted to mention to them that he seemed to be infatuated with Sarah, he always tries to sit near her at meetings or is trying to catch her attention, haven't you noticed?'

'Now you mention it, yes I have,' replied Rissa. 'I remember one time when he visited our house to discuss some church event he seemed to resent my presence. At the time I never thought anything about it and of course I've never seen Sarah treat him any differently to the last vicar.'

'My thoughts exactly so I didn't see the point in mentioning it to the police. I did mention that I was surprised he had left the village without telling anyone just before Easter,' said Mary. 'The police had no more questions, thanked me for my time and left. Just after they had gone the doorbell rang and that Susan Harvey, his sister was standing at the door. I can't say I particularly like her but I invited her in and asked if I could help. It seems that she wanted to know what I had said to the police and that she too was going to question everyone in the village. I didn't tell her much but I asked her some questions about her brother, she was very evasive. She left and I saw her going next door to see Jackie Shah.'

Rissa and Mary continued to talk about the missing vicar but neither of them could think of any reason for him to disappear. Rissa expressed her concern about there being no one to officiate at her wedding. Mary assured her granddaughter that he would turn up but also suggested that she contact the vicar of the next parish to see if he would be free that day. Rissa then bade her grandmother good-bye and returned home.

At Chadsbury Hall Rissa first of all went into

the kitchen and grabbed a glass and a bottle of chilled white wine out of the fridge. She then went up to her room, changed into a comfortable old pair of pyjamas and a dressing gown, poured herself a glass of wine and sat in an armchair. Taking the file of documents Anne had given her she rifled through the documents and found one pertaining to the De Montagu family of Chadsbury Hall in the 15th century. She settled down to read.

Kathryn de Montagu stood at the window of her bedroom and watched her husband as he rode off with only his dogs and his falcon for company. She turned from the window sighing and wondered how she was going to fill her day. Kathryn de Montagu was lonely and bored. She had lived at Chadsbury Hall for less than a year, marrying Thomas de Montagu in the summer of the previous year.

Although no one had been unkind to her they had made no attempt to include her in their lives. Thomas de Montagu was the local lord of the manor and he owned vast quantities of land including the village of Chadsbury Green about a mile from the Hall. He was much older than his young wife, a quiet studious man who liked his own company and spent many hours shut away in his room with his books or riding around his vast estate with only his hounds for company. He had lost his first wife after a long illness and had remarried for the sole purpose of begetting an heir. He was not unkind to his young wife but found her uninteresting and uneducated and he seldom talked to her, not even in the marriage bed. Their couplings were a duty that Kathryn had to endure; they were not pleasurable for either party, as Thomas de Montagu was an unadventurous lover with little regard for his wife's feelings.

Kathryn was 19 years old and she was unaccustomed to living in a large household with no nearby neighbours. She was the daughter of Richard and Mary Leys, a merchant in the local town of Kilborough. Until she had left to live at Chadsbury Hall she had lived in the small town house with her family helping her mother with the domestic chores. Her parents were very pleased when the local lord took his daughter to be his wife. From their infrequent visits to the Hall they knew she was unhappy but were unable to help her.

Kathryn sat down on her bed and thought back to the evening before. Henry and Francis Wodewarde, the local parish priest and his young nephew the monk had been guests at the dinner table. The conversation at the meal had been lively and including a discussion about the bible and other scholarly works. Kathryn had sat quietly throughout the meal giving little contribution to the conversation, as she understood little of what they discussed. Also seated at the table were Viola and Margaret de Montagu. Viola was Thomas's widowed mother who managed the household. Margaret was Thomas's unmarried sister, in her early thirties, and a scholar like her brother. Margaret was always busy with her studying or administering to the sick in the village, and found Kathryn to be rather pathetic and never had much to say to her.

During the meal the topic of Francis and his school was raised and Thomas de Montagu suggested that the young monk may like to visit the Hall and teach his wife Latin and French. Margaret had snorted but Francis had turned for the first time to look at Kathryn and in his quiet melodic voice asked her if she would like that. Kathryn had returned the look and studied the face of the young monk. What she saw was very pleasing and she agreed to his tutoring her without demur. Her husband was pleased and it was arranged that Francis would visit three afternoons a week.

As Kathryn sat on her bed there was a knock on the door and Viola de Montagu bustled into the room.

Viola was in her late sixties and had ably managed the domestic chores of Chadsbury Hall since marrying Thomas's father. She had continued in this role during all the time of Thomas's first marriage, his first wife had been sickly from the outset. Since the arrival of Kathryn, Viola had not encouraged Kathryn to help her but during dinner the evening before she had realised that it was about time Kathryn learnt how to manage the household.

Viola walked over to Kathryn and sat on the bed next to her.

'You can't spend the rest of your days moping around in here, it's about time you learnt how this house was run,' she said brusquely. Kathryn was startled but kept silent. 'I know I haven't been friendly since you came here but you need something to do and I won't live for ever,' she continued. 'As you are going to spend your afternoons with that monk I want you to spend every morning with me learning how we do things.'

Kathryn looked at the older woman and smiled.

'Thank you,' she said. Suddenly her life was improving.

'Well we can't sit here all day, there is the linen closet to check,' said Viola, standing up and marching out of the room. Kathryn also stood and happily followed her mother-in law.

Chapter 7

Susan Harvey was a very worried woman. When she found out that her brother had disappeared on the day he was going on retreat she had become greatly concerned. The evening before she had visited him and they had had an argument. He had suggested that perhaps it would be better that she didn't contact him in the near future and that he had plans which didn't include her. She had left him that night very angry and frustrated. The reason for her visit was to repeat her offer to come and be his companion in the village. This time instead of letting her down gently he had in no uncertain terms told her that she was not wanted. He had also hinted that his circumstances were soon to change and he hoped to have a companion in life. Susan was very puzzled by this, he had never mentioned he was seeing anyone, in fact she had never known of any woman in his life. She suspected he had had a serious relationship when he was at university but it had come to nothing and she remembered how distraught he had been at the time.

Susan was not happy with her life and resented everyone about her. When her parents had been killed she had just left school and had great plans for her future but with the death of her parents she had sacrificed these plans to take care of her brother in his school holidays. She trained as a librarian and took a job in a library in a small provincial town and there she had stayed. She was a very plain woman and found it difficult to make friends easily therefore her social life was very dull. She had hoped when Richard took on the parish of Chadsbury Green that he would welcome her to live with him and help in social aspects of the church. Although she was his sister Richard was aware of her social inadequacies and had never encouraged her to join in his life.

When she had visited Richard she had met the ladies of the church and had despised the young attractive ones especially Sarah Montague. She also found most of the older ones boring but in her imagination she saw herself in the role of popular assistant to the vicar.

Since finding out about Richards disappearance she had taken some leave owing to her and travelled to Chadsbury Green to stay at the vicarage to try to find out where her brother might be. Today she planned to visit his friends and neighbours and ask them questions even though she knew the police had already done so. She was just on her way to visit Dora and Edith Little that lived near to the vicarage. She remembered Dora as an old gossip but Edith was quieter than her sister was and Susan sensed that she had a malicious streak in her; if any-one knew anything about Richard they would. She arrived at their door just as the church clock struck eleven. Dora answered the door and beamed in delight when she saw their visitor.

'Oh do come in dear, what a lovely surprise, we do love to have visitors,' said Dora as she ushered Susan in to the sitting room. 'Edith, look who I found on our doorstep and she is just in time for coffee, and perhaps we could open that new packet of chocolate biscuits we just bought. Sit down there next to Edith and I will just go and make the coffee and bring the tray in.' And with that Dora left the room. Edith sat there not saying a word and so Susan said.

'Your sister certainly can talk, but it isn't her I wanted to speak to, I was wondering if you could help shed any light on the whereabouts of my brother?'

'What makes you think I can help,' said Edith.

'I've noticed on my previous visits that unlike your sister you don't say much but you always seem to be quietly observing people and assessing them. Rather like me,' Susan replied.

Edith understood immediately and said,

'Well, as you've asked me I shall tell you. On the afternoon when we were going to the retreat I saw Tom Montague leaving the vicarage slamming the door as he did so and cursing the vicar. He got in his car and raced out of the village at a breakneck speed. Perhaps you should ask questions at the Hall.' At that moment Dora entered the room with

65

a tray and Edith stopped talking. 'Here's the coffee, I'll put it down on that table next to you Susan if you could be so kind as to move those magazines dear,' said Dora. Susan did as she was asked and Dora put the tray down and handed the coffee round. 'There is sugar on the tray and also those nice chocolate biscuits I mentioned; please help yourself' continued Dora hardly pausing for breath. 'I hope you two have been having an interesting chat while I was out. I was only saying to Edith this morning how worried we were about your poor brother, dear, we do miss him so.' Susan interrupted and asked Dora.

'Have you any idea where he can have gone?'

'I have no idea, we have thought about it constantly but it just doesn't make sense he was so looking forward to his trip to the retreat with us. I was in town that day. I had gone in on the bus to do a bit of shopping. I left Edith at home but she is no wiser than I am,' Dora said. Susan looked at Edith but said nothing. She finished her coffee as Dora continued to chat about nothing important and when she got the chance Susan made her excuses and left.

As she hurried out of the door she wondered how Edith could live with the constant chatter of her sister. She had planned to visit Mary Montague but decided against this idea and instead went to the Angel for her lunch. Dawn Mallory's greeting was friendly and Susan ordered a fisherman's' pie and a glass of red wine. While she was waiting for the meal she tried to strike up a conversation with Dawn but the pub was busy and Dawn had her hands full with orders for food. Susan went and sat down and took a large mouthful of her drink. She surveyed the room but there was none that she recognised except for Dezi and Jackie Shah. Dezi noticed her and waved, he then turned to his wife spoke to her and they both crossed the bar towards Susan.

'May we join you?' he asked. 'There doesn't seem to be any familiar faces in here today'. Susan acquiesced and they both sat down. Dezi continued 'I have been at my warehouse this morning and when I came home I suggested to Jackie that we had lunch here, the food is always excellent.' Susan agreed about the food and she turned to Jackie and said,

'I am here for a few days to try and help find my brother, have you seen anything unusual at the vicarage?' Jackie looked at her husband but before she could speak he said laughingly with a hand on his wife's arm.

'Jackie never sees anything that goes on, she is always curled up reading a book or watching television. It took me all my time to persuade her to come out to lunch.' Jackie didn't say anything but just sat there looking down at her lap. Susan tried again to get Jackie to speak,

'We have something in common then, I am a librarian and I love books. What type of books do you like to read?' Jackie lifted her head and said in a very quiet voice.

'I like mysteries, thrillers and whodunits.' After that Jackie didn't say much but her husband talked incessantly in a loud voice about his wholesale grocers business and his plans for the future. Their meals arrived and Dezi bought another round of drinks. When Susan had finished her meal and got up to leave he said to her,

'I hope Richard returns before the cricket season starts. He's a good player and we shall miss him.'

Susan left the pub and walked across the green to the vicarage thinking what an odd couple the Shahs were. She let herself in and decided to spend an afternoon looking through Richards's papers in his study. Richard was very organised and she found it very easy to go through his desk and filing cabinet. She became quite engrossed in some of his documents, which were about his parishioners.

Susan was enjoying herself, she liked being nosy and delving into her brother's private life. When she had finished rummaging through the filing cabinet she started on the drawers of the desk. The bottom right hand draw was locked and she looked about for the key. She found it without difficulty where Richard had attempted to conceal it under the clock on the mantelpiece. She opened the drawer and found that all it contained was a scrapbook. She removed it excitedly and hurriedly flicked through it. She was amazed at what she found the scrapbook was full of newspaper clippings and pictures of Sarah Montague. Susan looked at them more closely and found that the cuttings went back over thirteen years starting with a picture of Sarah at some important charity lunch she had catered for in the city. Susan couldn't imagine why Richard would have this scrapbook in his desk but she knew what she had to do with it. She reached for the telephone and dialled the number of the police station.

Chapter 8

That same Saturday morning Rissa rose early, dressed in a navy trouser suit and hurried downstairs. She entered the kitchen, greeted Mrs White and poured herself some orange juice. Mrs White frowned when Rissa said that was all she was having for breakfast but didn't say anything. As Rissa left the house Lucy came running down the stairs and was greeted by the dogs at the foot of the stairs. Rissa told her to say goodbye to everyone for her and left by the front door and drove to Kilborough station. She parked her car, bought her ticket and went on to the platform. Fay, Simon's sister was already there waiting for her. As usual Fay looked stunning simply dressed in brown leather jacket and a short black velvet skirt. Her straight shoulder length hair was tucked neatly behind her ears.

'Hi, I hope you've remembered your credit cards,' was her greeting to Rissa. Rissa nodded and the two of them stepped on to the train and found two empty seats. They sat down and proceeded to make plans for their shopping trip to London. Rissa was hoping to buy some summer clothes for her honeymoon and she also wanted to collect some curtains she had on order. The furniture for the new house was either on order or had been donated from the attics of Chadsbury Hall. Rissa already had some bed linen and kitchen utensils and everything else they needed should be covered by wedding presents. Fay needed some shoes for the wedding but very little else.

Fay asked if they had managed to identify the skeleton yet and Rissa said no but they did think he might be a pilgrim. She then told Fay about how she had been learning about her family and how it used to be de Montagu. The train pulled into Liverpool Street station and the two girls headed for a coffee shop for coffee and a pastry before hitting the shops. They spent a pleasant morning around Oxford Street and Rissa purchased one or two items for her honeymoon including a new bikini, shorts and a couple of dresses for the evening. They also found some shoes for Fay and then stopped for lunch before continuing. In the afternoon Rissa bought Fay some pretty slides for her hair which they thought would go well with her bridesmaids outfit. Rissa continued to spend her money on clothes and finally they collected the curtains before struggling back to Liverpool Street Station with their purchases to catch the train home.

When they arrived at Kilsborough station Rissa offered to drop Fay off at her house. As they drove through the market square they passed Jake and Anne who were parking their motorbikes outside what Rissa assumed was Anne's flat. She sounded her horn and waved as she passed.

'Have you met Anne James yet, Fay?' asked Rissa.

'No I haven't, but Simon mentioned her to me,' replied Fay.

'I really like her; I thought we could ask her to my hen night, she doesn't know many people and it would give her a chance to meet some of our friends. Mind you she seems to be getting on well with Jake Allen. Didn't you have designs on him once?' enquired Rissa.

Fay retorted,

'We did have a very short fling but we were not really suited, I have stayed friends with him though and sometimes see him when I'm out with a crowd. Isn't he a little young for her?'

'It's not age that matters when you look like Jake,' laughed Rissa. 'Have you sorted out where we are going for my girls' night out?'

Fay had agreed to organise Rissa's hen night and as usual was leaving everything to the last minute. Rissa didn't want a large party, just a gathering of a few friends.

'I thought we could all go for a meal at that new Italian restaurant by the river, they say the waiters are very good looking with really neat bottoms and there is a small dance floor,' answered Fay. 'If you approve, I will book a table for the Tuesday before the wedding.'

'That sounds like a good idea; Simon and I have been meaning to try it out but never seem to find the time. Going with a crowd of women sounds so much better as I don't suppose Simon would appreciate the finer points of the Italian derriere,' Rissa agreed. 'Will you contact everyone or shall I?'

'It's OK I can do that this evening if you can give me Anne's number. I take it you will ask Sarah?'

They agreed on the guest list which included Jenny and Jane Allen plus three of Rissa's closest friends.

Rissa drove out to the home of the Middleton family, which was a large modern house in its own grounds, built on the outskirts of Kilborough. Fay asked Rissa in for a drink and Rissa agreed to a quick cup of tea. She was greeted warmly by Doreen Middleton her future mother-in-law and the three of them sat at the kitchen table and drank their tea.

Doreen Middleton was a homely woman who had spent most of her life tending to the needs of her family. Now as the family was leaving home she found she had time on her hands and she had recently taken up golf. She found that she enjoyed it and it meant that she could spend more time with her husband Jack. Jack also was happy with the arrangement and was planning a golfing holiday in Spain for them with two friends from the golf club.

Doreen was very excited about the trip, which was planned for early June, previously she had never joined her husband on his golfing trips but if this one was a success they planned to have many more.

Doreen asked to see what they had bought and Rissa was sent out to the car to return with her purchases. Doreen also asked how the garden design was coming along and promised to come and see it later that week. Rissa collected up her purchases and said that she must be heading back home. She told Fay not to forget the booking and set off home.

As she was driving towards Chadsbury Hall a police car turned out of the gates and passed her heading towards Kilborough. As it passed her she glanced inside and saw to her horror her father sitting on the back seat. He saw her as he passed and gave her a half-hearted wave. Rissa couldn't understand what was happening and she raced up the drive, leapt out of the car and rushed inside.

In the Hall she came across a very distraught scene, Sarah, Harry and Lucy were all in tears and Mrs White as white as her name was trying to comfort them. Rissa hurried over to her stepmother and put her arm around her.

'What's happened, I've just seen Daddy in a police car,' she said.

Sarah didn't reply but Mrs White said,

'You take Sarah into the sitting room and I will

look after these two,' and with that she took the children by the hand and led them into the kitchen. Rissa also took Sarah by the hand and they walked into the sitting room. She sat Sarah down on the sofa, poured them both a large gin and tonic and sat down beside her. Sarah took a sip of her drink and seemed to be regaining her composure.

'Can you tell me what's going on?' asked Rissa.

Sarah turned to her and said,

'They have taken your father in for questioning about the Vicar's disappearance. It seems someone has reported seeing him having a violent argument on the day he went missing and the police want to question him about it.'

'But what would Daddy have to argue with the Vicar about; they have always seemed to get on fine,' said a perplexed Rissa

'It's all to do with me, all my fault,' said Sarah, 'and it's a long story. If I told you from the beginning you may begin to understand why your father has been taken in for questioning.'

Sarah continued. 'As you know, my father was a history professor at Cambridge University. He was also assigned to be tutor to some of the students; one of these was Richard Harvey. All through my childhood I had grown used to these young men spending time in our home and joining in with our family activities. I was seventeen when Richard first visited our house. Richard was studying history and theology and he was twenty-one years old. He was a very quiet young man unused to the boisterous family life that we enjoyed. His parents had been anthropologists and spent most of their life abroad visiting their children rarely. Richard and his sister were sent to boarding school and spent most of their holidays with a variety of relations occasionally flying out to visit his parents in exotic locations. When Richard was just eleven years old his parents were killed in a plane crash and as his sister had by then left school he spent his future holidays with her. You have met her I believe; she is hardly a lively individual. Richard enjoyed spending time at our house and I suppose my mother felt sorry for him and always made him feel welcome. I was a popular outgoing teenager and always had one or two boyfriends in tow. That summer my mother invited Richard to spend some of the holidays with us at our holiday home on the Norfolk coast. The weather that summer was hot and sunny and we spent most of our day's outdoors, riding, swimming and sailing. Richard paid me a lot of attention and I was very flattered, as he was so much older than I was; I'm ashamed to admit it now but I flirted outrageously with him. One evening there was a storm and Richard and I were stranded in the boathouse. Like they tell it in all fictional romance stories, I ended up losing my virginity. I am not sure who seduced whom, as I wasn't the only one for who it was the first time. I found that I enjoyed it and over the summer we repeated the experience a number of times. By this time Richard was besotted with me and wanted to marry me. I am sorry to say I just laughed at him and when we returned home continued to see other boys. I don't think I intended to hurt him but I was young and just starting to experience life. All through the next year Richard pestered me, following me everywhere and watching my every move until finally I plucked up courage and told my mother all about it. I told my mother that Richard wasn't to blame for my losing my virginity but I couldn't handle his seriousness and persistence in wanting to marry me. My mother was very understanding and said that she would talk to my father. I had just completed my A levels and was going to college in London that Autumn, my parents arranged for me to spend the Summer in France with friends and I never saw Richard again until he came to Chadsbury Green.' At this point Sarah paused and looked at Rissa. 'Are you shocked?' She asked.

Rissa shook her head.

'No, but I can see how this must have helped you with your dealings with me.'

Sarah continued. 'After completing my catering course I started to work in the city and it was there that I met and fell in love with your father. Who I have been faithful to all through our marriage.

When Richard came to Chadsbury Green I was surprised but not unduly worried and treated him just like I would treat anyone in his position. I assumed that he had got over me but that was not the case. About a month ago I called in on him to discuss some charity do I was organising and he poured his heart out to me. Telling me that he still loved me and that he would never find anyone else. He also said that he knew I felt the same and that we should run away together. He then produced a scrapbook that was full of pictures and newspaper cuttings of me. Not that there was many, but there were photographs of me at functions in the city, my wedding day and pictures from our local paper. I must admit I was quite unnerved but managed to leave his house and come straight home to tell Tom all about it.'

Sarah saw Rissa's horrified face.

'You mean to say that our vicar has an obsession about you? But he seems so normal; mind you granny and I were saying last night that we had noticed how he looks at you,' said Rissa.

'Really, I hope no one else noticed,' said Sarah. 'To continue, your father was very angry and said that we should go to the bishop but I persuaded him to calm down and hoped it would blow over. Your father needed no convincing that I no longer had any feelings for Richard, but unfortunately it didn't end there. On the day Richard disappeared

Tom had a phone call from him saying he had some urgent church business to discuss. Your father went over there just before lunch in all innocence and was confronted by an almost manic Richard. Richard told him that I had agreed to leave Tom and that Richard and I would be leaving that night. Tom knew this couldn't be true but I'm afraid he lost his temper said a few choice words to Richard, left the vicarage slamming the door and raced back here. Edith Little was walking up the vicarage drive as he left the house, which is why the police are now questioning your father.'

'But that's terrible,' said Rissa 'I mean, what do they think he has done to Richard, killed him and buried the body?' Rissa stopped speaking when she saw the anguished look on Sarah's face. 'I am sure Daddy will convince the police that it was just a silly argument. No one could suspect him of doing any harm to anyone.'

Sarah smiled weakly.

'You and I know that, but they would reckon he had good cause especially if they believe I was having an affair with Richard. Can you imagine the gossips in the village - they are going to dine out on this tale for months. There is still the problem of Richards's whereabouts - it certainly looks suspicious, and I don't suppose they have any other suspects. Richard just wasn't the type to have many enemies. Putting aside his silly infatuation with me he was, sorry is, a good man and an excellent vicar.'

Rissa agreed with her and spent the next hour with her comforting her and trying to talk about other things. They heard the telephone and a few moments later Mrs White knocked on the sitting room door and entered.

'That was Tom on the telephone, he says that the police have finished questioning him for now and he is allowed home and could someone pick him up,' she said.

Rissa jumped to her feet.

'I will go and collect him, I suggest you Sarah go and have a nice hot bath and Mrs White could you arrange a nice supper for Sarah and my father?'

'That sounds like a good idea, I have just given the children egg and chips and they would like to see you Sarah before they go upstairs,' replied Mrs White. 'Perhaps Rissa you would like to eat with me on your return?'

Rissa agreed, kissed Sarah and went to collect her father.

When she had gone Sarah got to her feet and went through to the kitchen to find the children, she sat down with them and tried to explain what was happening. She told them that Rissa had gone to collect their father and he would come and see them before they went to sleep. She then wearily went up the stairs to soak in a long hot bath. She ran the bath and emptied half a jar of bath oil into it; she lay in the water and thought about Richard and all the problems he had caused her. She admitted that at seventeen she had found him attractive and certainly had no regrets about her summer fling, what she did regret was that she hadn't been mature enough to cope with Richard when he became demanding and serious. She was sorry that he hadn't found himself a wife, one that would have suited his calling but she admitted to herself that even if she had never met Tom she could never have being a vicar's wife. She emptied her bath, dried herself and dressed in a pair of loose trousers and top and lay down on the bed to wait for her husband.

Rissa drove as fast as she could to the police station and when she arrived she found her father waiting for her. She hugged him fiercely and led him to the car and on the return journey they both sat very quietly saying little. When they arrived home Rissa turned to her father and said, 'when you are ready I am sure you will tell me all about it but right now you need Sarah and Sarah needs you.' And with that she went into the kitchen leaving her father to go upstairs to the bedroom he shared with his wife.

As he entered the bedroom Sarah got up and ran into his arms and he held her tight.

'When I went off in that police car I thought I would never come home, never see the children again but worst of all never hold you again,' said Tom, the tears streaming down his cheeks.

Sarah just held on to him and said,

'I love you,' repeating the words again and again. After some time had passed she worked her way free of his embrace and asked him if he would go and say goodnight to the children and that she would go and collect a tray from Mrs White. Tom left to see Harry and Lucy and Sarah fetched a tray with a bottle of wine and some sandwiches to their bedroom.

When Tom returned she told him to sit down and tell her all about it but instead he raised her to her feet and kissed her. The kisses become passionate and urgent and Sarah returned them with the same passion until they were all but tearing each other's clothes off. They both staggered to the bed removing their clothes as they went. They continued to explore each other as they lay on the bed each knowing what the other desired after being married for so long until finally they both paused and looked into each other's eyes. Tom raised himself above Sarah and plunged into her with a great force thrusting in and out until he was spent and she was writhing in ecstasy. He then slumped on top of her and closed his eyes; she again whispered her love, and they went to sleep wrapped in each other's arms.

Chapter 9

The next morning Sarah woke up to the sun streaming in to the bedroom. She looked around and saw their clothes strewn around the bedroom and the untouched tray on the table and all of yesterday came flooding back. She turned to look down at her husband who still asleep and snoring softly. He looked so vulnerable and innocent lying there and Sarah bent down and gently brushed the hair from his face. As she did so he woke up and looked up at her he lifted up his arms and pulled her down to him and made love to her very gently.

When Rissa came down the stairs to breakfast she was surprised to hear the sounds of laughter coming from the small dining room. She entered and was greeted by four happy smiling faces. Her father looked happier and more relaxed than she had seen him in ages and he and Sarah who sat at the other end of the table were laughing at the antics of Harry and Lucy who were having a funny face competition. Rissa went to her father and kissed him on the cheek and said,

'Was yesterday all a dream?'

Her father frowned and replied.

'No, but Sarah and I think everything should carry on as normal,' and he looked at his wife as he spoke and smiled.

'I hardly call this normal,' laughed Rissa. 'You

normally have your head in the paper and just growl at everyone.' They all laughed.

'We hope that you are coming to church with us this morning Rissa, I would like the whole family to be there, a united front, show everyone that we have nothing to hide.' Tom said.

Rissa agreed, and she sat down to eat her breakfast and joined in with her siblings in making funny faces.

The family assembled at the main door in their Sunday best and Tom went to collect the car, a large Mercedes. They all piled in and drove to church. Tom parked the car close to the church and the family trooped into the church greeting people as they passed them. Some of the villagers just stared but others returned the cheery greetings. It was obvious that everyone knew of Tom's visit to the police station. Harry and Lucy were on their best behaviour in the church and when the service was finished they were allowed to let of steam in the graveyard with the Allen twins but they had strict instructions to keep clean. Tom and Sarah stood outside the church and passed the time of the day with some of the villagers but not one of them mentioned the vicar until Susan Harvey came out of the church. She strode over to Tom pushing past Julian Simpson Talbot who he was talking to and said rudely.

'I didn't expect to see you here; I thought you

would still be in gaol explaining what you had done with my brother.' There was a loud gasp from those in hearing distance but Tom calmly replied.

'I have answered the police questions to their satisfaction and I am now trying to continue with my life. I am sorry about your brother and I am as puzzled as you are as to his whereabouts.' He then turned his back on her and continued his conversation with Julian about the organ. Susan Harvey was fuming but no one took much notice of her and she stormed off.

Rissa came over to Tom and Sarah.

'Granny has been speaking to Reverend Arden who took the service. It seems they are old friends and he is standing in for Richard until he returns' explained Rissa. 'He has kindly agreed to officiate at the wedding if Richard hasn't returned.' As she finished speaking her grandmother and William Arden walked across the grass towards them.

'Tom, you remember William, he used to be the vicar here when you were still a boy, it seems that he has retired to the area and the church use him to officiate when there is a need.' said Mary Montague. Introductions were made and Sarah invited him for lunch, which William Arden accepted. Tom said that he would have a pint in the pub and it was finally arranged that Rissa and Mary would return to the Hall with the children. Sarah, Harry and William Arden would have a drink before William drove them back to the Hall for lunch.

Tom and Sarah strolled across to the pub with the elderly vicar. He remembered the Angel from when he had been in the village in the 1960's and was interested to see how it had changed. They entered and were greeted cheerily by John Mallory.

'Good to see you squire, and it's always a pleasure to see the beautiful Sarah, what will you be having?' It was decided that the two men would have a pint of bitter and Sarah settled for a white wine spritzer. The pub was fairly busy with the usual Sunday crowd and a number of visitors out for a days run in the country and there to sample Dawn Mallory's Sunday roast. They collected their drinks and Tom asked if William would like to sit but he said no he preferred to stand at the bar. They stood and chatted, Tom, with his arm about his wife's shoulder. George Allen came over to join them.

'I am sorry to hear about last night, I hope everything is OK now Tom?' he said.

Tom assured him that it was but didn't mention why he had been called in, he suspected the whole village was dying to know and no doubt they would in the not too distant future. Dezi Shah came in to the bar and he slapped Tom on the back, Tom winced.

'Hear you had a run in with the police last night, what did you do, murder Richard?' Dezi said and laughed jovially. Tom didn't reply but George did.

'I don't think that is very funny, do you Dezi?'
He then turned back to talk to William Arden, making sure Dezi knew he was been ignored, and Dezi retreated down the bar. Sarah smiled gratefully at George. They finished their drinks and left the Angel. No one else had really mentioned Tom's visit to the police station but he was quite sure there would be much speculation when they left. As William Arden drove them home Tom explained to him why the police had suspected him of foul play and he hoped that Rissa had had chance to talk to her grandmother about it.

They arrived home to find the whole family already seated at the table waiting for them. They sat down and Mrs White brought in a large joint of beef for Tom to carve and they ate this with Yorkshire pudding, roast potatoes, parsnips and sprouts. Conversation at the table was lively and William Arden was an excellent dinner guest relating amusing stories from his life as a vicar. The meal finished with a gooseberry fool and the children went off to play while the adults repaired to the formal drawing room for coffee.

Over coffee, Tom reassured his mother that there was nothing for her to worry about and the conversation turned to the discovery of the body at Brook House. Mary and William expressed an interest in the old documents that Rissa had, and she brought them down to show them.

Kathryn de Montagu sat, fiddling with the belt of her gown, in the small parlour or solar waiting for Francis Wodewarde to arrive. Today was her first lesson with the young monk and she was very nervous. As she waited she thought back over the last few days in which for the first time since she had arrived at Chadsbury Hall she had been fully occupied. From that first morning when Viola, her mother-in-law had visited her she had been occupied with helping Viola and learning about the day to day running of the Hall. She had found it to be not that very much different from at home but on a much grander scale. Viola was a good teacher and Kathryn was enjoying the hours she spent with her. This morning they had spent time in the larder making an inventory of all the preserves and dried goods that were stored there. Kathryn was amazed at the quantity of food and she expressed an interest in learning how to make the different preserves and Viola had said that she would show her in time. Viola was very methodical and she wrote everything down. She expected the servants to work hard and didn't allow any shoddiness but she was a fair mistress and the servants respected her for it. Kathryn hoped that in time they would respect her too but she had to admit that some of them made her very nervous. This morning William Aleyn, the reeve had been in the kitchen with Roger Tyler, the bailiff and she had felt uneasy under their constant stares. Roger Tyler was getting on in years and he was relying more and more on William Aleyn to help him with the running of the vast estate. William Aleyn was popular in the village but he made Kathryn uncomfortable. He was always very polite but his manner was unctuous and he was always trying to ingratiate himself with his peers.

As Kathryn continued with her musings there was a knock on the door and Francis Wodewarde entered the room. Kathryn stood up but neither of them said anything and for the first few moments they both stared nervously at each other. Kathryn remembering her manners asked the young monk to sit down; he thanked her and sat on a chair at the opposite end of the room. The silence continued until Francis cleared his throat and said,

'I really don't know where to begin, your husband asked me to come here to try and teach you French and Latin, but I don't have any idea about what you already know.'

'I really don't know much at all, and living here with my husband and his sister makes me feel that I know even less. If you could help me so that I can converse with my husband I would be happy,' she replied, not looking at him but down at her lap still playing with the belt of her dress.

The young monk realised that she was more nervous than he was and said,

'Perhaps today you can tell me about yourself, what you did as a child, what you enjoy and then maybe we can see where to begin.'

Kathryn looked up at him and he smiled at her.

'I really don't know what to say.' She replied.

'Start with your life as a child,' he suggested. Kathryn continued to play with her belt but started to speak, quietly at first but as she grew more confident her voice became louder.

'I had a very happy childhood; I lived in the town with my parents and younger brother and sister. I did go to school sometimes but most of the time was spent playing with my brother and sister and helping my mother around the house. It wasn't a house like this we only had one servant.'

Francis asked her questions about her family and began to draw her out of her shell. 'I remember the times I liked the most were when my father had the time to take us out for the day and we would take the pony and trap out of the town and into the country. I loved to smell the flowers and hear the birds singing,' she continued. Francis asked her if she liked poetry and she said that she didn't really know any. He suggested that on his next visit he would read her some poetry and maybe translate it into French so she could start to learn the language.

The afternoon flew by and when it was time for Francis to leave Kathryn went with him to the door of the parlour to say goodbye and then he left.

Kathryn sat down and thought about her afternoon, she had enjoyed herself, it had been nice to talk to someone nearer her own age and sometimes she had even forgotten that he was a monk. She looked forward to the next afternoon when he would visit again.

Chapter 10

Francis left the Hall to walk back to the village; he was deep in thought and didn't notice William Aleyn until he collided with him.

'Here! Watch where you're going,' snapped William and then seeing who it was modified his tone and said, 'I am sorry sir, it was my fault. I must have been in your way.' Surprised, Francis muttered that it was he who had been in the wrong and he hurried on his way thinking that there was something about the reeve that he didn't much like. As he neared the village he saw Molly Makepeace, the alehouse keeper's daughter. She was sitting outside the alehouse on a bench plucking a chicken. She looked up as he passed and gave him a wave and a large wink; he nodded at her and carried on. Molly turned to her father, who had just come outside and said,

'It's a pity that one is a monk, he's right handsome and I am sure would be a bit of fun.' Her father looked at her fondly and pinched her cheek lightly; she was a good daughter and worked hard in the alehouse. She was also very attractive which was good for business and she had all the village lads, not to mention quite a few of the men, chasing after her, and she flirted with them outrageously.

'I thought you were walking out with young Robert Aleyn,' he said to her.

'I can still look,' she replied cheekily, thinking not only of Robert but also of his father who she was sure wanted her.

Francis turned into the churchyard and entered the church where he knelt in front of the altar and prayed. Since meeting Kathryn de Montagu he had for the first time had doubts about his vow of chastity and he was horrified that he could have these thoughts about a young married lady. He knelt in front of the altar for over an hour and then he got up from his knees and went home to his uncle's house.

Henry and Francis sat down to a light evening meal and as it was a warm evening Henry suggested that they went for a walk. They strolled through the village discussing the day's events but Francis was very reticent about his first lesson with Kathryn only saying that it had gone well. Henry suggested that they started asking the villagers if they would be willing for their children to attend lessons with Francis as they had previously planned. Francis was still enthusiastic about this project and as they passed the alehouse he turned to his uncle and said,

'Maybe we could have a glass of ale. We could also ask some of the villagers in there what they think about a school.' As the local priest Henry Wodewarde did not frequent the alehouse on a regular basis but on the odd occasion he had dropped in and he was always received warmly.

'I think that might be a good idea,' he replied, and they turned to enter the door to the alehouse.

It was not a large establishment, just a small room that was part of the house, but it was a place where the villagers could meet and relax after a hard days work spending their precious money on ale.

As Henry and Francis entered everyone stopped talking and turned to see who it was. The silence was broken by Joshua Makepeace saying.

'Well, its not often we see you in here but sit down and I'll pour you a drink.' Molly brought the frothing jugs of ale over to them and they supped at their drinks enjoying the warm brew. They looked around the room and saw a number of their parishioners including Edward Smithson, the blacksmith and William Aleyn. Edward Smithson was a large well-muscled man with long black hair and a beard; he was very popular amongst his peers, not afraid to speak his mind. Henry turned to Francis and said

'Now Edward would be the one to talk to about a school; he has eight children and people listen to him, if we could get him to agree to sending some of his children for lessons then others would soon follow'. Henry cleared his throat and called over to Edward. 'Edward, we wondered if you had time to talk to us we have a proposition that we would like to put to you.' Edward looked surprised but in his loud booming voice said,

'What on earth do you want to talk to me about it; I hope you have no complaints about attendance at church?'

Henry replied,

'No. This is more to do with your children and what my young nephew can do for them.' Edward came and sat with them intrigued by the priest's words. Henry continued. 'Francis and I thought it would be a good idea if the children of the village were taught to read and write, and Francis has volunteered to start a small school in the village. We thought that some of your children might like to attend.' Edward looked at the priest with astonishment.

'But reading and writing is for the lords and ladies, not for us simple folk.'

Henry went on to explain.

'That isn't true; there is no reason why the children of the village shouldn't benefit from learning their letters and some simple arithmetic, it can do no harm. It may help them when they are older if they decide do to do something other than work on the land.' Edward thought about this and could see the sense in this, he himself could read and write a little but he knew most of the other villagers couldn't. He also understood that jobs like Roger Tyler's, the bailiff, needed someone who could read and write.

'I am prepared to give it a go if it doesn't inter-fere with their chores at home and in the fields,' he said. Francis joined in the conversation and they talked about what the children would learn and it was agreed that the six eldest children would come to the priest's house for two hours, two mornings a week. Edward agreed that if he liked the arrange-ment he would persuade others to send their chil-dren.

Edward left them and they finished their ale, they stood up to take their leave but on the way out of the door. William Aleyn stopped them.

'I heard you talking about teaching the children to read and write - I would like some of mine to learn. I can read and write myself but have never had the time to teach my children. Robert the eld-est is sixteen but he is not too old to learn and I have plans for him and his brothers.' Francis said that Robert and his two younger brothers could join the blacksmith's children and then he and his uncle left the alehouse and returned home to bed.

William Aleyn smiled to himself; he had great plans for his family. He intended to be the next bailiff and wanted his son to follow on after him. He knew that Roger Tyler would recommend him to the post but he needed to impress the master and his mother to be sure of getting the job. He decid-ed that he must spend more time at the Hall making himself indispensable to everyone there. His thoughts turned to more immediate matters, that of chatting up Molly Makepeace, he knew that she had been walking out with his son, Robert but he also knew that Robert wasn't the first and he had decided to try her out himself.

Leering as he spoke he said to her. 'Well then Molly, how are you finding young Robert, a bit wet behind the ears for you I would have thought?'

'What he lacks in experience he makes up for in enthusiasm,' she replied. 'He's a handsome lad, takes after his father I can see.'

'Oh, he does that alright, but if you are going to become part of the family I really need to see what you are made of,' William retorted. Molly giggled and looked William up and down and then she whispered.

'Why don't I show you round the back of the church when I've finished up here?' And with a wiggle of her hips she flounced off to help her father.

William was a thickset stocky man but he had always had a way with women. Although he had been married for over eighteen years to Anne he enjoyed dallying with other women and there were one or two maidens in the village who had married in haste due to being pregnant with a child of Williams. Molly was a lively intelligent girl and he could see she would be a good wife to Robert and he could see no harm in trying her out first. He drank his ale and went to sit in the graveyard to wait for Molly.

Molly finished clearing up, told her father she was going for a walk before going to bed and set out for the churchyard. Molly enjoyed the company of men. Her father was very lenient with her and was well aware that she was no longer a virgin. He didn't worry too much about her and as long as she didn't cause problems in the village he wasn't going to interfere. Molly was still only fifteen but she realised that it was about time she settled down and Robert Aleyn seemed an ideal candidate. She knew his father was ambitious and as Roberts wife life would be better than it was for most of the women in the village. She had no twinges of guilt about meeting William, she considered it to be a bit of fun and as long as Robert never knew there shouldn't be a problem.

It was quiet in the churchyard and although the moon was out she couldn't spot William. She was therefore taken by surprise when a hand encircled her around the waist from behind and whispered in her ear for her to be quiet. The arm that held her spun her round and she saw that it was William. He pulled her behind the church and pushed her up against the wall. She leaned against the wall as he pawed at her dress kissing her as he did so. He smelt of ale and stale sweat and she lowered her hand and felt him hard against her. Molly laughed softly.

'Not so fast, let me help,' and as she said this she undid the bodice of her dress so that her milky white breasts spilled out. William grabbed at them groaning in delight and as he played with them Molly undid the ties of his trousers and let hem fall to the floor, she then lifted up her skirts and taking hold of his throbbing member pushed it against herself. William was very strong and he let go of her breasts and lifted her up grabbing hold of her buttocks, squeezing them as he did so. Molly wrapped her legs around his waist as he entered her and as he thrust in and out she moaned with pleasure and grabbed at his hair. William finished in one final shudder and they both fell to the ground panting. They lay there for awhile with their eyes closed and then William heard the cracking of a twig; he opened his eyes and saw the figure of a man standing at the corner of the church. The moonlight reflecting off his tonsured head. The man was looking straight at them but he didn't say anything he just turned and walked away.

Chapter 11

The next morning William Aleyn was walking, with his eldest son, through the village. They were going to spend the morning working on their small plot of land where they grew the vegetables and crops for their own use. William intended to leave Robert there all day but he had some jobs to attend to at the Hall in the afternoon. As they passed the church they met Francis Wodewarde and William said a nervous good morning. Francis returned the greeting giving William a disdainful look as he did so and then continued on his way. William breathed a sigh of relief, he had guessed that the young monk had recognised him last night and he was now praying fervently that he wouldn't mention their encounter to anyone, especially his wife or his son Robert. He thought that maybe if he met Francis on his own he might speak to him about it. His thoughts turned to the previous night and Molly. She had certainly been lively he thought and he was looking forward to future encounters. His thoughts were interrupted by his son, who said,

'Father, you know I have been seeing Molly Makepeace these last few weeks? Well, we have decided that we would like to marry.' William had been expecting this and he would certainly welcome Molly as a daughter-in-law, especially if she still let him pleasure her. He stopped walking and spoke to his son.

'That's good news lad, I have no objection to you marrying the lass but where will you live? It will be a bit cramped at home.'

'Molly said that we could live with her father; there is plenty of room and she would still be able to help him with his work,' replied Robert. William could see no objection to this; in fact it would give them a bit more space in their own home.

'Well, when we get home this evening we will have a word with your mother and then go and see the priest about the wedding. Mind you, I want you to still have those lessons with the monk I told you about,' William said. Robert agreed and they set off again to the fields.

When William and Robert had passed him by, Francis thought back to what he had seen the night before. He had told his uncle he was going to the church to pray and check that there had been no candles left burning. When he had arrived there he had heard noises around the back of the church and he had gone to investigate. The scene he came across was not what he had expected and he stood there for some time watching the coupling of William and Molly. To his shame he had found it arousing and he was disturbed by his reaction. Part of him was horrified at what he had seen between a young girl and a married man but he was also appalled by his body's reaction. He had spent most of the night in the church on his knees praying for forgiveness. As a young boy Francis and the other novices at the monastery had played with themselves and each other but he had never made love to a woman and it wasn't until very recently that he had even thought about women in that way. He shook his head to try and rid them of lewd thoughts and went on into the village to pay a visit to the elderly Mistress Dove.

Mistress Dove was what would be considered as the local wise woman. She had a vast knowledge of herbs and she had spent her life curing the minor ailments of her fellow villagers. She also assisted the women during childbirth and most of the villagers had been brought in to the world with the help of Mistress Dove. She was an old woman now, very frail but still with a keen mind and Francis enjoyed visiting her. When he arrived he found that she already had a visitor, Margaret de Montagu.

Margaret was an unusual woman not typical of her class. She was unmarried, scholarly and spent her days in the village administering to the sick. She had been spending a lot of time with Mistress Dove learning about herbs and their uses. Her brother had not objected to this but he had put his foot down when she had expressed an interest in midwifery.

'Good morning Lady Margaret and Mistress Dove, I hope that I find you well,' said Francis.

Mistress Dove answered, her voice still strong,

'I'm fine in my mind it is just my body that lets me down. I don't think I will be much longer for this world; I'll soon be needing your uncle's help.' Francis assured the old lady that he was sure she had many more years on God's Earth, but looking at her frail body he doubted it.

'I came on my uncle's behalf to say mass for you,' he continued. The old lady laughed and said,

'You can say it if you want but I would rather talk about more interesting things; I hear that you are going to start a school in the village.'

'Yes I am, we just hope that it will be a success. Lord de Montagu has given his consent and I am going to start soon with the Aleyn and Smithson children,' he told her. Margaret interrupted a smile on her plain face.

'Will you need any assistance? I would really like to help. ' She looked at him eagerly. Francis studied her; she was a tall, homely woman, severely dressed but her smile lit up her face making her almost beautiful. On previous occasions when he had met her he had found her to be haughty and he had thought her dull.

'Until I have started the lessons I won't know how many children there will be. If it is a success I will probably need some help and when I return to the monastery someone will have to take my place,' he answered. 'If you are willing I would gladly accept your offer of help but you would need to ask your brother's permission.'

'I shall speak to him tonight,' Margaret said excitedly. Mistress Dove interjected

'I am not sure that teaching the children is a good idea, it may give them ideas above their station and make them discontented.' Margaret and Francis both vehemently disagreed with the old woman, who laughed and said,

'We shall see.'

Francis said goodbye and left the house to return to his uncles for his midday meal. When he saw Henry he told him about his conversation with Margaret de Montagu and also remembered to tell him that he didn't think that Mistress Dove would live much longer. When they had finished their meal Francis set off for the Hall for his second lesson with Kathryn.

He met William Aleyn for the second time that day; he too was on his way to Chadsbury Hall. They walked along the lane together although Francis would have preferred his own company. William tried to start a conversation and said,

'I am needed to help with repairing the roof on the stables at the Hall; we all have to work there when we are summoned. I spend a lot of my time there now as Roger Tyler is getting on in years and needs all the help he can get. I am hoping my role there may be more permanent in the near future. I know that Roger Tyler is going to recommend me to replace him, but it wouldn't do any harm if others put in a good word for me.' Francis didn't take the hint but just nodded. William continued 'I had a bit of good news this morning, my son Robert is hoping to wed Molly Makepeace she should make him a good wife.' At this Francis stopped and looked at the older man in astonishment.

'That's odd, I saw Molly last night and the man she was with looked more like you than Robert, maybe you would like to explain it to me?' William tried to look apologetic but inside he was seething,

'Oh that, it was only a bit of fun, you won't tell anyone will you?' he whined. Francis looked at him in disgust,

'No, I won't tell anyone what I saw but I suggest you think very carefully about what you did and pray for forgiveness. If you want to be bailiff they will expect you to be honest and reliable.' William nodded his head vigorously and thanked Francis saying.

'Thank you sir, there won't be a second time.' William then strode off to the stables cursing to himself.

Francis continued on the main door to the Hall thinking that he didn't trust William Aleyn and he was sure he had made an enemy.

He was met at the entrance by a servant who escorted him through to Kathryn. She seemed pleased to see him and asked him to sit down.

'No, it's such a lovely day I thought we could go for a walk and we can learn the names of things in French as we walk,' Francis suggested. Kathryn was delighted and said that she would need to collect her cloak, which she did and they set off for a walk. They spent an enjoyable afternoon walking in the grounds of the hall. They even laughed about Kathryn's deplorable pronunciation but by the end of the afternoon she had learnt a number of words and Francis complemented her on her memory. Kathryn blushed and said it was time to return home.

They walked past the stables; they were deep in conversation and didn't notice William Aleyn on the stable roof watching them. As he looked down on the two young people he wondered what they were talking about. 'It would do no harm to keep an eye on them in the future,' he mused. 'It might be of some advantage to me.'

Chapter 12

After Francis had left Mistress Dove's cottage, Mistress Dove and Margaret shared a simple meal and then Margaret stayed on listening to Mistress Dove talking about herbs and their uses. The cottage was small, only two rooms, but one of these was full of various powders and lotions which Mistress Dove had made from local plants. Mistress Dove had shown Margaret how to make some of these preparations and Margaret had written down all she was told. Mistress Dove was very impressed by this as all her recipes were in her head and had been passed down to her from her mother.

'You'll not forget what I've told you seeing as how you are recording it.' Mistress Dove said. 'When I first started out I made plenty of mistakes because I hadn't remembered what my mother had told me.'

'You see there is some merit in reading and writing,' Margaret said. 'I shall be able to take my journal home with me and try and recreate some of these remedies at home without your help.'

'The trouble is,' said Mistress Dove. 'You are not always going to be here and the women still need someone to help with childbirth, we will have to think of someone to help you. There is Jane Smithson the blacksmith's wife, a strong woman. She has eight children of her own and I only helped her with one of them. Which reminds me, can you visit her on your way home, her youngest has a bad cough and I have some ointment you could rub on her chest.'

'Yes, I can do that and I could also ask her if she wants to help with the midwifery,' replied Margaret. They agreed that this was a good idea and Margaret left the frail old woman, collected her horse and led it up through the village to the blacksmiths.

She tied the mare up outside the blacksmith's yard and Edward Smithson came out of the smithy to greet her.

'Do you need a new shoe, my lady?' he called to her. 'I can fit it in now if you want.'

'No, it's not you I've come to see,' she said. 'But I was hoping to have a word with your wife. Mistress Dove sent me over to look at the cough your little girl has.'

'Oh right,' said Edward. 'You'll find her round by the house'. The villagers were used to Margaret's coming and goings in the village and had learnt not to stand on ceremony with her when she visited. Margaret stepped warily through the smith's yard to the house behind it. Jane Smithson saw her coming and she greeted her at the door.

'Welcome Lady Margaret, how can I help?' she asked. Margaret explained that she had come with some ointment from Mistress Dove for Jane's youngest child. The little girl was standing behind her mother clutching at her skirts. Margaret bent down to the child and said,

'Hello and what is your name?' The small girl looked at the beautifully dressed stranger in awe.

'Mary,' she replied, and as she spoke her small frail body bent double with an attack of coughing.

'Well, Mary, I may be able to help you with that cough I have brought some nice smelling ointment for you which we will rub in to your chest.' Margaret said to the little girl holding out her hand. Shyly Mary took the proffered hand and Jane led the way into the house so that Margaret could apply the ointment. While Margaret was attending to Mary she said to Jane, 'Mistress Dove said that you might be able to help with the delivery of the babies in the village. As you know Mistress Dove is not able to get out much now and she has been teaching me all about medicine. I am not allowed to help with childbirth and someone is needed to take over from Mistress Dove.' Jane thought for a moment and said,

'I am very busy at home but I would be only too pleased to help.' Margaret said she was pleased and suggested that Jane went to see Mistress Dove. She gave the ointment for Mary's chest to her mother and went to collect her horse for the ride home.

Riding was one of Margaret's great pleasures and when she left the village she urged her horse into a canter. The horse responded and they flew down the lane to the Hall. She rode into the yard and dismounted from the horse and handed him over to the groom. She crept into the house hoping she wouldn't meet her mother before she had changed her mud stained gown. As she was reached the bottom of stairs she heard voices and hurried quickly up the stairs. Margaret changed her dress and tidied her hair and then went in search of her brother. As she was passing the front door it opened and Kathryn entered the house, her face flushed from her walk with Francis.

'Hello Margaret, have you had a pleasant day?' Kathryn asked. Margaret was surprised as Kathryn hardly ever started a conversation,

'Yes, I have just spent the day in the village with Mistress Dove,' she answered.

'Oh yes, Francis - I mean Brother Francis, said that he had seen you there,' Kathryn's said. 'He was telling me about his plans for a school and also that you are interested in helping him. I do so admire you both you are so clever.' Margaret didn't know what to say - she had never seen Kathryn so animated.

'If Thomas gives his permission then yes I shall certainly help Brother Francis. How are your lessons coming along?' Kathryn blushed and said. 'Today we went for a walk and I learnt the French names for some of the things that we saw. I am really enjoying it.' Margaret nodded and continued on in search of her brother wondering what had brought about the change in her normally quiet sister-in-law.

She found her brother in his room going through the estates books, he was swearing to himself. When his sister entered the room he scowled and said,

'What do you want? Perhaps you can help me with these ledgers - I can't read my own writing.' Margaret hurried to his side and together they deciphered his scrawl. Thomas thanked her and shut the book. 'Well what can I do for you?' he said.

'I have been speaking to Brother Francis who incidentally seems to be making headway with Kathryn, I saw her just now and I have never seen her so animated. Anyway he says that you have given him permission to teach some of the village children to read and write and I have offered to help him,' Margaret said looking at her brother pleadingly. 'He said he would welcome my assistance but only with your permission.' Thomas looked at his sister and said,

'I suppose there is no chance of you leaving here and getting married so you may as well teach in the village.' Margaret thanked her brother and he offered her a seat and a glass of wine and they sat together in companionable silence.

That evening there was just the family for dinner; Thomas, his wife, mother and sister. Usually when this was the case the meal was eaten in relative silence with short conversations between Thomas and his sister or his mother. Tonight however Thomas made an effort to talk to his wife and was pleasantly surprised by the answers to his questions.

'Margaret told me that your first lessons with Brother Francis have taken place. I trust that you have learnt something?' he said to his wife.

'Yes,' she said, looking directly at her husband, 'I have learnt a few words in French. Brother Francis is a good teacher and very patient with me. I am sure he will make a success of a school in the village.' Thomas asked a few more questions and was pleased with the replies. Viola joined in the conversation and said,

'Kathryn has also been very busy this week with me. Once I have her properly trained I am sure she will be able to run this household efficiently and I can retire and sit quietly in my room,' she smiled at Kathryn.

'Oh no!' Kathryn exclaimed. 'It will be years before I can manage on my own.'

'I have no intention of stopping just yet,' the older woman said. The meal finished and Kathryn rose to go to her room. She bid everyone goodnight and as she was leaving the room her husband called after her,

'Don't go to sleep my dear, I shall be coming to

see you before I retire.' Kathryn slowly climbed the stairs, sighing as she did so. She understood the meaning of Sir Thomas's words and although she knew that it was her duty she dreaded his nightly visits.

Viola and Margaret also said goodnight to Sir Thomas and left him at the table finishing his wine. He sat there for a long time thinking of his wife and how the last few days she had spent in the company of his mother and Francis Wodewarde had changed her. He hoped the change in her might also be visible tonight. He visited his young wife regularly as he wanted a son and heir, but he had derived little pleasure from their couplings. They had been no more than a way to beget an heir and relieve his natural urges. He finished his wine and walked up the stairs to Kathryn's bedroom.

He opened the door and found his young wife sitting on the edge of the bed in a white night gown combing her hair. She was looking very beautiful and he felt a stirring in his loins. At the sound of her husband entering the room Kathryn sighed inwardly but she stopped combing her hair and smiled at her husband. He gestured at her to get into bed and he sat on the edge and pulled off his boots and removed his clothes. He then got into bed beside her and started to fumble with the ties at the neck of her gown. When he had released the ties he pulled the neck of her gown down to reveal her small pert creamy white breasts which he kneaded with one hand while he pulled her gown up from the bottom with the other. He positioned himself on top of her and entered her with difficulty and then he kissed her, his sour wine smelling breath making her want to retch. Most nights Kathryn just lay there while thinking of other things while he went about his business but tonight was different and he could sense it. As she lay there her thoughts turned to Francis and as her husband continued with his inexpert lovemaking instead of pain she felt wetness between her legs. She wriggled slightly beneath his body and Thomas responded by finishing quickly and slumping down on top of her. He rolled off her, turned on his side away from her and was soon sound asleep and snoring. Kathryn lay there for a long time, feeling slightly frustrated, and then she too fell asleep thinking of Francis.

Chapter 13

Rissa was up bright and early on Monday morning as she intended to spend the morning working at the stables. As it was raining she was dressed appropriately and put on her riding mac before leaving the house. She set off for the stables in her car, the windscreen wipers on full. 'Well at least I won't be tempted to go riding,' she thought.

She arrived at the stables to find Jenny and the other two girls busy mucking out the horses; she greeted them and hurried in to the office. She sat in her chair behind her desk and set to work. About two hours later Jenny popped her head around the door with a mug of coffee and asked if Rissa needed anything doing. Rissa looked at her watch and was surprised to find how quickly the morning had disappeared. 'Thanks for the coffee Jenny, I needed that' she said.

'I have just been checking the diary and we are expecting a new horse from Mrs Talbot-Booth tomorrow, can you make sure the corner box is ready for her? I seem to have got on top of the paperwork and I shall finish here at lunchtime. If the weather improves make sure all the horses are exercised and also we are expecting a delivery of feed this afternoon.'

'OK,' said Jenny, 'I think we can handle that. The weather is looking brighter so with any luck we will be able to exercise some of the horses this afternoon. Totally unrelated but much more interesting, Jake didn't come home on Saturday night!' and before Rissa could say anything she left the office. Rissa made some phone calls and continued to clear her desk. At about one o clock, Rissa switched off her computer stood up stretching as she did so and left the office. That morning she had collected some sandwiches and a thermos from Mrs White and she was intending to have her lunch at Brook House. She pulled into the drive of the house to find it deserted; obviously the workman had gone for their lunch. She went inside and into the dining room where she sat on the floor and ate her lunch. When she had finished she walked quickly around the house to see how they were progressing.

It seemed that all the plumbing, wiring and decorating were complete. She was pleased about this as the carpet fitters were due in on Wednesday and she hoped to be arranging furniture and hanging curtains next week.

She went outside and looked at the patio, which seemed to be nowhere near finished. Just as she was about to leave George and Jake Allen returned from lunch and George assured her that he would finish the patio by the end of that week. He also said that all the remaining work after that would be nearly finished by her wedding day and when she returned from her honeymoon there would be no evidence that they had ever been there. Rissa laughed.

'I will believe that when I see it. Anyway I must dash I have arranged to see Anne James at the museum.'

Jake said, 'Send her my love,' and blushed. Rissa set off for Kilborough thinking that she must ask Anne how the romance was progressing.

She pulled in to the museum car park, locked the car and entered the museum. While she was waiting for Anne she picked up a leaflet on the history of Kilborough; she was so engrossed that she didn't hear Anne arrive. They greeted each other and Rissa followed Anne up to her office. Anne was again dressed in a large baggy sweater but his time she wore it with a short black skirt, thick black tights and her lace up boots.

'Are you cold?' teased Rissa, pointing at the sweater.

'The council have declared that it's officially summer and so they have turned the heating off. In the mornings it can be very cold in here, and I do feel the cold,' said Anne indignantly.

'I was only joking,' said Rissa. 'I too have been stuck in the office all morning but if anything mine can be too warm. I've just seen Jake and he sends his love. Did you have a nice day out with him on Saturday? We saw you on our way back from

London.'

'Yes, we had a great time,' answered Anne. 'We rode a long way; Jake must have showed me all of the local beauty spots. We had a nice pub lunch at some village near a river - I forget where - and then we came back here. I ached all over and after a nice hot bath I cooked Jake a meal and we listened to music.'

'And?' Rissa said.

'And what?' asked Anne.

'I know Jake didn't go home that night' she answered. Anne blushed and said hotly,

'This is worse than being at University; can't I do anything without the whole world knowing?' Rissa laughed and said,

'I'm afraid there are no secrets in Chadsbury Green, I should know, I have had to contend with it all of my life. Try not to let it get to you.'

'Jake is really nice,' Anne said, 'I am enjoying his company. Wednesday night I am going to have supper with his parents. Did you know his mother is tracing their family tree? Jake thought I might be interested to see how she is getting on and he thought I might be able to help her.'

'Yes, I did know', said Rissa. 'She went on a course with my grandmother who is also tracing my ancestors, I had forgotten all about it until I was showing granny the documents you loaned me. I let her borrow them for a day or so to help her fill in some gaps in the family tree. She suggested I called round sometime to look at it.'

'You never know, yours or Jake's ancestors might have known our pilgrim when he was alive,' said Anne. 'Which brings us to the main reason for your visit. I have spoken to the expert on old bones and he is very interested and plans to come and look at the bones. I will let you know what he says.'

'Why do you call him The Pilgrim?' asked Rissa.

'Well, as I said before, he had a pilgrims' badge with him and also a silver cross and as we don't know his name I thought we could call him 'The Pilgrim.' I have cleaned the cross up as it was heavily discoloured. It has given me no clues, as it is very simple - the sort a priest or a monk might wear. I have also cleaned up the coins and one of them is definitely a medieval half-groat of the 15th century, and the other two coins are of a similar age, which would mean that the pilgrim would have been alive sometime in the 1400s. Would you like to see the cross and coins?' Rissa said that she would and Anne took them out of her drawer and showed them to her. Now that they had been restored Rissa could just make out the markings on the coins, she was fascinated. Anne returned the finds to her drawer. 'At the moment, I can't really tell you anymore. Perhaps we should ask your grandmother and Mrs Allen for a copy of their work so that we could try and correlate the two.' Rissa agreed that it sounded like a good idea and said she mustn't keep Anne from her work any longer. Just before she left Anne said 'Fay Middleton phoned me last night and invited me to your hen night. Thank you for asking me I am really looking forward to it. Finding the pilgrim has certainly improved my social life.' Rissa said goodbye and left for home.

Rissa drove straight home and her heart nearly stopped beating when she saw a police car parked outside the house. Not again, she thought, I hope they haven't come for daddy again. She rushed out of the car her heart thumping and raced up the steps to the front door. It opened just as she reached it and Harry raced down the steps followed by the dogs, shouting at her.

'Guess what sis, Nicola, Sophie and I have found a dead body!' He was hopping from one foot to the other unable to suppress his excitement. Rissa immediately thought of Richard and hoped that the body that they had found was not his. Harry continued, 'we were playing football and the ball went into a ditch by the side of the field and that's when we found him, Mr Shah. He was covered in mud and blood and we could tell he was dead. We didn't touch him and while I stayed and guarded the body Sophie and Nicola ran to their house and their mother called the police. A police car came with flashing lights and when the policemen saw the body they called on their radio and two more police cars and an ambulance came. It was ace!' As he paused for breath Rissa heard voices and her father and Sergeant Bridges appeared in the doorway.

'We seem to have seen a lot of your family these last few days and never in pleasant circumstances,' the sergeant said. He looked at Harry, 'Now don't you worry about what you have seen today young man and if you can think of anything else you need to tell us just let me know'. He shook hands with Tom and Rissa and left in his police car.

'Harry has just been telling me about Dezi Shah, dad, isn't it awful?' said Rissa.

'Yes, it is terrible and they are treating it as a murder enquiry. They will be questioning everyone in the village. They are also concerned that it may be related to Richards's disappearance. Sergeant Bridges brought Hary home and naturally he asked me some questions about my whereabouts yesterday evening. I told him that I was here with the family and Mrs White corroborated my story. I don't think I am the Number One suspect but I am probably high on their list' he said ruefully, and then he put his arm around his son and daughters' shoulders and they all went inside.

Chapter 14

That night the Angel in Chadsbury Green was full, everyone was there discussing the latest tragedy in the village and the disruption it was causing. The football pitch had been cordoned off and there had been a constant stream of police cars in and out of the village since the children had found the body. John and Dawn Mallory were rushed off their feet serving drinks to the locals and providing meals for the press, a television crew and a number of people who had just come to have a look. Simon Middleton had called in for a drink on his way up to see Rissa and he had been persuaded by the Mallorys to help out behind the bar. He phoned Rissa and told her what he was doing and he suggested that she joined him there.

Rissa arrived at the pub and pushed her way through the throng to the bar. Dawn saw her and suggested she joined Simon on the other side of the bar; this she did and she too was soon busy helping serve drinks. It was not her first time; she had helped out on previous occasions and quite liked working behind the bar. She didn't get much of a chance to talk to Simon but they managed the odd word. Julian Simpson –Talbot stood at the bar and he said that his wife had gone round to see Jackie Shah but the police wouldn't let her in and they had said that Jackie was expecting some of her family down from Leicester that evening. George and Jake Allen stood next to him and they said that Mrs Allen had also wanted to visit Jackie but she had her hands full with the twins. Nicola seemed to be unaffected by what they had found but Sophie was very upset and there had been tears at bedtime. Mrs Allen was very worried and the police had said that they could arrange trauma counselling for the children if they thought they needed it. George asked Rissa how Harry was and she said that he was much the same as Nicola but she wasn't so sure how long the euphoria would last. Just at that moment a reporter from the local paper pushed his way towards the bar and stood next to George.

'I couldn't help overhearing your conversation,' he said to George. 'We would like to interview the children who found the body and I believe that you are their father.' George looked at the reporter a mixture of horror and anger on his face.

'No you bloody well can't. I suppose you will be asking for their pictures with the body next?' George shouted at the reporter

'Steady on mate, I'm only trying to do my job,' the reporter said, as he hurriedly backed away from George, seeing the anger in the other man's eyes. He turned away and went to find someone else to pester leaving George to be calmed down by his son and his friends.

'Dad, he didn't mean any harm,' said Jake.

'Well I never have liked to see that type of reporting in the newspapers and the thought of seeing the twins in the paper associated with a murder horrifies with me,' George said, calming down. 'Mind you, Nicola and Harry would probably love it.'

'I had better phone home and warn them about reporters,' Rissa said, 'I never thought about them wanting to see the children.'

'I'm afraid the press are going to be in the village for some time,' interjected Julian. 'If they also get wind of the vicar's disappearance it could get worse.' 'That could mean trouble for my father,' Rissa thought, and went to call home.

Simon went to collect some glasses and he saw Susan Harvey was sitting at a table deep in conversation with the local television crew. He returned to the bar and said to Julian and George,

'They already know about Richard, Miss Harvey is talking to them now.' They all turned and looked over at the corner where Susan was sitting.

'She's a troublemaker that one is,' said George. 'I can understand she is upset about her brother but there is probably a simple explanation. We really don't need someone poking around in our business.' He finished his drink and he and Jake left the bar. Rissa returned and they told her about Susan, she was visibly worried - her father could do without the publicity. The crowd in the pub gradually got smaller and at 10 o'clock John Mallory thanked Simon and Rissa for their help and said he could cope without them. Rissa suggested they went to Brook House for a chat and a cuddle and Simon quickly agreed. They both drove their cars to their house and Rissa unlocked the door and they went inside. She turned on a light in the dining room and they sat down on the floor. Simon told Rissa all about his climbing weekend and she told him all about her weekend including her father's arrest. Simon assured her that there was nothing to worry about, he was sure everything would soon be resolved. He put her arm around her and pulled her close. They sat for a long time together just enjoying each others company and then Simon suggested that perhaps they should go and find the cushions and make themselves more comfortable. He pulled her to her feet and led her upstairs.

Rissa and Simon had fallen asleep at Brook House and woke up with the dawn. They dressed themselves quickly and returned to their respective homes for a shower and breakfast. As Simon drove through the village he saw that there was still a large police presence in the village. The football pitch was still cordoned off and the police were searching the surrounding area for evidence. As he drove past the Shahs' house he saw a large black Mercedes in the drive and he wondered to whom it belonged.

Jackie Shah had not slept all night she had just

lain there thinking. She saw Simon driving out of the village as she was walking past the landing window on the way to the bathroom. She went downstairs and found her two brothers, Arnie and Jo dozing in chairs in the living room. They had arrived the night before with her sister-in law and today she was expecting her sister and her husband to join them. Her two brothers were older than she was; they were very successful businessmen in Leicester and owned a lot of property. They were very powerful men within their own community.

As she entered the room the older one stirred in his chair, saw his sister and asked her how she was. Jackie said that she was fine and she was just about to make some tea and would he like some. He said yes and she went through into the kitchen and put the kettle on.

Jackie's thoughts turned to the afternoon before. When the body had been found the police had come and broke the news to her. They had been very kind and a young policewoman had sat with her until her brothers had arrived. The police had then left saying that they would question her in the morning. She had sat with her brothers late into the night rehearsing what she would say to the police when they interviewed her. They assured her that if she stuck to her story she would have nothing to worry about.

They drank their tea and Jackie's sister-in-law,

Meena came downstairs and she made them all breakfast, not that Jackie could eat much. At about nine o'clock the doorbell rang and Meena answered the door. On the doorstep were two plain-clothes policemen.

'May we come in? We've come to see Mrs Shah.,' said the older one. Meena opened the door wider and the policeman followed her in to the sitting room. The policemen introduced themselves and they were offered a seat. Meena left the room but Jackie's brothers said they would stay with their sister.

'We have a few questions to ask you, Mrs Shah,' said Chief Inspector Lacy 'and my colleague Detective Inspector Williams will be taking some notes. We would like us to tell us of your movements on Sunday.' Jackie cleared her throat and glanced nervously at her brother Arnie and said,

'On Sunday morning we lay in bed until quite late reading the papers. We got up and while I was preparing lunch Dezi visited the pub for a drink. We had a late lunch and as it was a nice day Dezi persuaded me to go for a walk. That evening I watched television and Dezi did some paperwork in his office. I went to bed about 10 p.m. and Dezi said he was going out for some fresh air before coming to bed. I read for about an hour and then turned my light off and went to sleep. '

'Did you hear Mr Shah return?' Lacy asked.

'No, but then I sleep soundly,' she looked embarrassed 'Dezi sometimes sleeps in the spare room so that he won't disturb me.'

'You are saying that he slept in the spare room?' queried Lacy.

'Well, when I woke up the next morning he wasn't in the house, so I assumed he must have done and then gone to work early,' she replied.

'Can you think of anyone who would want to harm your husband; friends or business associates?' he continued.

'No, I can't think of anyone, but then I don't know many of his business colleagues,' Jackie said.

'Well, thank you for your time Mrs Shah, it is still early days yet and we will probably want to question you again.'

'We were hoping to take our sister back home to Leicester with us' Arnie interrupted.

'I am sorry but that would not be possible, we need her to stay here for the foreseeable future. Will someone be able to stay with you Mrs Shah?' said Lacy.

'I will stay for a few days and her sister can come down,' Arnie replied for her.

Meena escorted the two policemen to the door and they went out to their car.

'What did you make of that then, Dave?' Chief Inspector Lacy asked his younger colleague.

'I'm not quite sure; Mrs Shah was just too calm

128

as if she was relieved that her husband was dead. It was a right funny set up if you ask me; something wasn't right in that marriage. How many women do you know who just assume their husbands slept in the spare room and went to work early? I certainly think we need to look at Mrs Shah and her brothers more closely.'

'I agree with you,' Roger Lacy said.' I would like you to get on to Leicester and see if they have anything on Mrs Shah's brothers. It's a pity we haven't found the murder weapon yet, we shall just have to keep looking. Meanwhile we need to arrange to visit every house in the village and ask if they saw anything suspicious on Sunday night or Monday morning. I will meet you in the pub at lunchtime, the landlord of the pub may be able to help - they usually can.'

They got into the car and drove to the village hall which had been turned into the incident room for this enquiry. The hall was a hive of activity and telephones and computers were being installed. Dave Williams sat at the desk allocated to him and started to make phone calls to investigate the background of Jackie Shah's brothers, Arnie and Jo Patel. Meanwhile Lacy asked one of his men to organise the questioning of everyone in the village and then he went out to the scene of the crime.

He arrived there and found the forensic science team packing up their equipment; they said that they had sufficient samples from the area to do an analysis. Police officers were still searching the surrounding area but had not found a murder weapon. Roger Lacy returned to the village hall to talk to his team.

The key personnel involved in the investigation were assembled at the village hall and Lacy posted guards at the entrances to ensure there were no uninvited guests.

Lacy addressed his investigation team. 'Yesterday afternoon a body was found in a ditch by the football pitch in Chadsbury Green. We have established that the victim is Dezi Shah, a resident of this village and the time of death was between 10pm on Sunday evening and 2am Monday morning,' the Chief Inspector told his staff. 'The victim had been stabbed a number of times in the chest but no weapon has yet been found. So far we have no witnesses and no major suspects although we cannot rule out the wife of the victim. Have you any questions?'

'Are we treating this as a separate case to that of Richard Harvey, the vicar?' asked Sergeant Bridges.

'At this time Richard Harvey is just listed as missing and we are not linking the two incidents' Lacy answered. 'We are now going to question everyone in the village about their movements between the times of 10p.m. and 2 a.m. and we will reconvene here this afternoon to go over their statements.'

As everyone dispersed Roger Lacy called Sergeant Bridges over.

'You seem familiar with most of the people living in this area; I would like you to accompany me to Chadsbury Hall to question Tom Montague' he said.

Roger Lacy drove up to the Hall to question everyone there. They found Tom and Sarah in and also Mrs White. They all provided alibis for each other for the night in question. The policemen then drove to the livery stables to question Rissa and she also corroborated her family's story. While they were there Sergeant Bridges asked if they could speak to Jenny Allen but she said that she had gone to bed early that night and not heard a thing. Sergeant Bridges drove Lacy back to the village and dropped him off at the pub where he was meeting Dave Williams.

Williams was already at the bar-drinking half a pint of bitter and talking to John and Dawn Mallory.

'Hello, Chief Inspector, I would like you to meet John Mallory the landlord and his wife Dawn. What would you like to drink?' he asked.

'The same as you I think' said Roger, and he nodded to John and Dawn Mallory.

'I have been asking John and Dawn if they noticed anything unusual on Sunday evening but they say it was very quiet' said Dave.

'That's right' John said joining in. 'We normally are quiet on a Sunday evening, most of our Sunday trade is at lunchtime. We only had one customer in when we closed the bar at 10.30 p.m. and Dawn and I were able to have an early night for a change. I was locked up down here by 11p.m.'

'What can you tell me about Dezi Shah did he come in here often?' asked Roger.

'Oh yes, Dezi was a frequent visitor to the pub, he didn't drink a lot but he liked to talk to people,' said John.

'Did he have any enemies that you know of?' continued the Chief Inspector.

'No, I wouldn't say he had any enemies,' John said slowly.

'But he wasn't popular.' His wife interrupted him. 'He tried really hard to join in. He was too pushy and loud in contrast to his wife who was so quiet, we all felt sorry for her. I am sorry he is dead but I doubt if he will be missed in the village except when there is a cricket match.'

'I don't like to admit it but my wife is right; I didn't like the man and neither did many of my customers, but I don't think any of them hated him enough to kill him,' said John.

'Did he ever bring any business colleagues into the pub?' persisted Roger Lacy. They both shook their heads. The policemen finished their drinks and walked back to the village hall. Leicester had been in contact while they were out and they had faxed over some information on the Patel brothers. Both of the brothers had a record for fraud and Arnie had also been suspected of GBH but it had never been proved.

By about 3 o'clock the Chief Inspector had all the statements from the villagers on his desk and he and Dave Williams were sorting through them. Most of the villagers had nothing to say but they found two that were of interest.

'Read this one sir,' said Williams. 'It is the statement of the Shahs neighbour, Mrs Montague.'

Roger Lacy read it. Mary Montague had gone to bed early on Sunday evening but she had woken up at about 2 am when she heard the noise of a car outside. She had gone to the bathroom and on her return looked out of her bedroom window. She had seen a large dark car parked outside the Shahs and two men standing beside the boot, which was open.

'I see what you mean,' said Roger. 'You and I need to visit this lady and ask her some more questions.'

'The other statement that was of interest was that of Jake Allen. He had been returning from Kilborough in the early hours of the morning on his motorbike when a large dark car had shot passed him and nearly knocked him off his bike. He recognised the car as a Mercedes!'

'Are you thinking what I am thinking?' Williams asked his boss.

'I would imagine so. It looks like one of the Patel brothers was here early Sunday morning. I think we need to question them and also arrange for a search warrant to go over the Shahs' house,' replied Lacy.

There was a sudden commotion outside the village hall and a young uniformed policeman rushed into the hall. His face was flushed and he was breathless from running.

'Sir, we have found a knife and they are bringing it in now,' he said panting.

Roger Lacy looked at the young eager policeman and said,

'Well that is good news, but haven't you heard of radios, lad?'

The young policemen blushed and apologised.

Two young detectives then entered the hall and one of them held up a plastic bag for the chief inspector to see. Inside was a large kitchen knife!

Chapter 15

On Tuesday evening Mary Montague telephoned Chadsbury Hall and asked to speak to Rissa.

'Rissa, can you come round tomorrow morning?' she asked. 'I gave a statement to the police this morning and it seems that they want to interview me again. I would prefer to have some company when they come.'

'Of course I can come granny,' Rissa replied. 'But wouldn't you prefer daddy or Sarah?'

'No, I think you would be less threatening,' her grandmother said.

Rissa laughed.

'I have to go to Brook House to check on the carpet fitters, shall I bring a packed lunch and then after the interview we can both go there and have a picnic?'

'That sounds like a lovely idea. The police are coming at 10 a.m. so I shall expect you before then.' Mary said and she rang off.

Rissa arrived at her grandmother's just after ten. She managed to park her car off the road and noticed there were two large cars at the Shahs.'

'Hello granny,' she said kissing Mary on the cheek. 'How are you this morning?'

'I'm a bit worried about why the police want to see me again, I don't want to get Jackie into any trouble, she seems so nice,' said Mary

'What do you mean?' Rissa asked. 'Surely they don't suspect her!'

'I don't know, but I told them I saw a car outside her house very early on Monday morning and it looked very like that big black one out there now. I tried to see her yesterday but she has her family with her and they said she doesn't want visitors.' Mary said.

Rissa looked at her grandmother and suddenly realised that she was getting old; she squeezed her hand and said reassuringly.

'Don't worry, I will be here.' At that moment the doorbell rang and Rissa went to answer it. Chief Inspector Lacy and Detective Inspector Williams were standing there. Behind them the lane was filled with police cars and Rissa saw at lest eight policemen walking up to the Shahs' front door.

'Hello again,' she said. 'I take it there are just two of you?'

'Hello Miss Montague,' said Dave Williams. Rissa took them through in to the glassed in porch overlooking the garden and then went to help her grandmother carry in a tray with coffee on it. She introduced the policemen and passed the coffee round and they all sat down.

'Mrs Montague, we are grateful that you could see us this morning. We just want to check some details of you statement that you gave our officer yesterday.' Chief Inspector Lacy said.

'Anything I can do to help,' said Mary. 'My granddaughter is here to keep me company, I hope you don't mind'.

'Not at all' he replied. 'If you could repeat what you told the young constable about the car, to us.'

'As I said, yesterday I woke up in the night and needed to go to the bathroom.' Although Mary was nervous she spoke clearly. 'I looked at the small clock next to my bed and saw it was just after 2 am. I went to the bathroom and before I got back into bed I looked out of my bedroom window as I had thought I heard a car. My bedroom window overlooks the lane at the front. I saw a large dark car outside next door and I could see two people standing by the car. The boot was open. I thought no more about it and went back to sleep.'

'That's very interesting,' the Chief Inspector said. 'Were you able to recognise the car or the two people?'

'It was quite dark and I couldn't recognise the two men, but the car looked very similar to the black one that has been parked outside Mrs Shah's since Monday evening,' she answered.

'You say that it was two men standing by the car?' he asked.

'Yes, now I think about it I am sure that they were men,' she replied.

'Was the car there when you got up in the morning?' he continued.

'No, the car had gone'.

'Well you have been very helpful and we probably won't have to trouble you again, Mrs Montague,' said Roger Lacy.

'Can you tell us what is happening next door?' Rissa asked. 'I saw all the activity as you entered the house just now.'

'All that I can say for now is that we are searching the Shah residence and Mrs Shah and her brothers are helping us with our enquiries,' he answered. Lacy and Williams finished their coffee and got up to leave. Rissa showed them out and as she did so she saw Jackie Shah and her two brothers being escorted to a police car.

'Granny, they have just taken Jackie off in a police car,' she reported to her grandmother.

'Oh dear,' said Mary. 'I hope they don't find that poor girl guilty of anything.'

'Let's change the subject,' said Rissa. 'I was hoping that you could show me how you are progressing with the family tree.'

Mary's eyes lit up as she spoke.

'Now that is a good idea, you clear the coffee cups up and I will go and get it.'

Rissa washed up the coffee cups and they sat down and looked at Mary's work.

'The last two centuries were relatively easy,' said Mary.' It became more difficult as we went further back through the centuries. Those documents you gave me are going to be a big help. I have glanced at them and can see that Chadsbury Hall was in existence as far back as the Domesday Book. It was owned by the de Montagu family from which I deduce we descend.' Mary said.

'That's really interesting,' said Rissa. 'Have you found the names of the family living in the 15th century yet, the time when the owner of the skeleton probably died?'

'No but I am sure I can work it out with time. It can be very confusing with all the different branches of the family. I am trying to trace a direct line through the centuries of those who lived at the Hall.' Mary answered. 'We could spend some time looking through the records now if you can spare the time.'

Rissa looked at her watch and said, 'As long as we are up at Brook House before noon, I don't see why not.'

Viola was in the kitchen discussing the next few days' meals with the cook. She had arranged to meet Kathryn there and they were going to spend the morning bottling and preserving fruits that had recently been picked. It was now early summer and the next few months would be very busy at the Hall and in the village. It was a time when food was plentiful and fresh but it was also necessary to ensure that enough food was preserved and stored for the winter.

Viola was pleased with the way Kathryn had developed in the past few weeks. She had been a willing pupil but Viola had also found her to be pleasant company and she was enjoying teaching the younger girl everything that she knew about running the household. Soon, thought Viola, she will be able to manage on her own without me. This thought was not altogether displeasing as Viola was finding that the demands on her were beginning to take their toll physically. She was no longer able to run up and down the stairs like she used to. Kathryn still lacked confidence when giving orders to the servants but Viola had noticed an improvement. Still, she thought, I hope to be here for a good few years yet and so I will be able to help her.

Kathryn came running into the room.

'Sorry I am late, but I was speaking to Thomas,' she said breathlessly. 'He is going into town today and he asked me if I had any messages for my parents. I asked him if they could come and visit for a few days and he said Yes.' Kathryn was smiling at the thought of seeing her parents again.

Viola thought she certainly is changing; a few weeks ago she wouldn't have dared ask my son for anything.

'I am sure you will enjoy their visit and I will be able to tell your mother how much help you have been to me,' said Viola. Viola liked Mary Leys; on their infrequent visits she had found Mrs Leys to be a down to earth dependable woman. Mary had confided in Viola that she was concerned for her daughter and it was this chat that had prompted Viola to make an effort with Kathryn. She was glad she had and she could see the mother's qualities emerging in the daughter. 'Enough of this idle chatter, we must get to work, we have a lot to do,' and with that the two ladies together with the cook and kitchen maid went about preparing the fruit for bottling. They worked hard all morning and by the lunchtime the kitchen maid was carrying numerous jars of fruit into the larder for storing. As Thomas was out all day and Margaret was in the village, Viola asked the cook to provide a cold meal for her and Kathryn to be eaten in the small parlour.

Viola was thankful to be sitting down after their morning's exertions and she and Kathryn enjoyed a light meal of bread and cold meat.

'I think I might lie down for awhile this afternoon. Are you seeing Brother Francis today Kathryn?' asked Viola?

'Yes, I am, he should be here soon.' Kathryn blushed at the thought of seeing him again. Viola noticed the high colour in daughter-in-law's cheeks but did not comment. 'You had better go and get ready then,' she said, and Kathryn left the room. When she had left Viola pondered on Kathryn's

141

reaction to the mentioning of the young monks name. She decided that she must keep a closer eye on Francis and Kathryn. She had seen with her own eyes the results of his teachings but she was concerned that their relationship was turning into more than that of pupil and teacher. She was a practical woman and knew that her son was not easy to live with but Kathryn was his wife and a De Montagu and as such she had a duty. She wondered about speaking to Kathryn and then thought maybe it would be better if she spoke to Kathryn's mother first. She sighed and lifted herself out of the chair and slowly made her way to her room to lie down.

Chapter 16

Francis hurried up the lane from the village to Chadsbury Hall. He was looking forward to seeing Kathryn. They had spent many afternoons over the last few weeks closeted together in the small parlour. He had found Kathryn to be a gifted student and her spoken French was improving every day. She was also learning to read and write in Latin in which she was progressing well but it was Kathryn the woman that Francis was looking forward to seeing. When they were apart he thought constantly of her, her perfume, the way she laughed and even the rustle of her skirts. Francis realised that he was in love. He felt guilty about his feelings, he knew that they were a sin and doubly so because he was a monk and she a married woman but he couldn't help himself. He spent many hours on his knees praying and he worked hard teaching the village children but he couldn't keep her out of his mind. He lived for those few precious hours when he could be alone with her. At their last meeting he had suggested that today they went for a walk in the fields and he knew that he would speak to her of his feelings. He could wait no longer.

Kathryn sat at the small table in her room brushing her hair; she plaited it in two long plaits and coiled it around her head, and her thoughts were of Francis. In the last few weeks she had grown very fond of him and thought of him in her every waking moment. She was glad that she had so much to do in the house with Viola as she found that when she was not busy time dragged slowly as she waited for her next meeting with Francis. She had found the lessons to be very interesting and was surprised at how easy the work was but she was sure that it was because of the teacher. She wanted to please him. Her relationship with her husband was a lot easier now and she was able to converse with him without him becoming impatient. She was so much more confident and she knew that this confidence stemmed from her friendship with Francis. She admitted to herself that she was falling in love.

Francis arrived at the Hall and a servant let him in and showed him through into the parlour. He waited for Kathryn impatiently pacing the floor not wanting them to waste a minute of their time together. The door opened and she entered.

'Good day Brother Francis,' she said.

'Hello Lady Kathryn,' he replied. 'It is a lovely day; shall we go for a walk as we planned?' She agreed and they left the Hall quickly and walked out into the lane and set off in the opposite direction to the village. They talked as they walked and Kathryn asked how his small school was progressing.

'It is too early to say yet,' he said. 'The pupils are

eager enough but I am finding that they don't always attend their lessons. When I ask why they say that they have more important work to do for their parents.'

'Well, it is a busy time of the year,' said Kathryn. 'Perhaps you will find it easier in the winter.'

'That is probably true but my time here must end here before the end of the year and I had hoped to achieve something by then.'

'You will be leaving us?' said Kathryn. She stopped walking and turned to him. 'But why must you leave so soon?'

'It was only intended that I stay for a year before I returned to the monastery,' he said quietly, not looking at her.

'But can't you change your mind and stay and help your uncle?' She said, her voice sounding distressed.

'It's not that easy. Shall we walk in the woods?' he said abruptly, changing the subject. She nodded her head and they turned off the lane and made their way across the field to a large wood. As they were entering the wood Kathryn stumbled and Francis put out his hand to steady her. He did not let go but held her hand for a long time and then slowly brought it to his lips and kissed it. Kathryn did not say anything but just stood there looking at him. Before he could think about his actions he took hold of her other hand and pulled her towards him. He then let go of her hands and put his arms around her waist and kissed her on the lips. At first she did not respond and then she reached up and put her arms around his neck and returned his kiss. He could feel her heart beating beneath her dress and he could feel himself stirring beneath his habit. They broke apart and looked at each other with longing. Without saying a word Kathryn took his hand and led him deep into the woods. It was gloomy and quiet in the woods and they could hear their own footsteps as they walked through the undergrowth. They came across a small clearing where the light filtered through the trees and here they stopped. Neither of them moved initially and it was Kathryn who again took the lead; she led him to a fallen tree trunk and they sat down. Kathryn cupped his face in her hands and kissed him. Francis responded and pulled her closer, his hands roaming over the bodice of her dress. Their kisses became more ardent until both of them were breathing heavily with desire. Kathryn pushed his hands away and stood up; slowly she undid the front of her dress from top to bottom and let it fall to the ground. Underneath she wore only a pale under dress and he could the see outline of her small breasts and her erect nipples beneath the fabric. He groaned loudly and fell to his knees in front of her and held her close his face between her thighs. Kathryn bent her head and kissed the top of his tonsured head holding him closer until she could feel his warm breath on her. Francis looked up at Kathryn and saw that he was trembling with desire. He released her and she lay down on the ground opening her arms to him. He bent over, his hands moving over her body and then he lifted the hem of her dress and put his hand between her thighs. He could feel the tight curls of her pubic hair and the wetness between her legs. He stroked the inside of her thighs and he lowered his face to explore the secret entrance to her body with his lips and tongue. Kathryn gave a cry of agonised pleasure and her hips rotated in response to his probing tongue.

'Make love to me Francis,' she cried. He straddled her lifting his habit as he did so and tried to enter her, but he fumbled in his excitement and inexperience and Kathryn took hold of him and guided him into her. The pleasure he felt was indescribable and he thrust himself deep within her. A cry escaped her throat and he smothered it to silence by covering her mouth with hers. He finished quickly but she too felt a small burst of pleasure. Francis rolled off her and they lay side by side panting. They lay in silence listening to the breeze through the trees and Francis reached for Kathryn's hand and held it. He turned onto one side to gaze at her and saw a tear rolling down her cheek.

'Why do you cry, my love' he said. 'Did I hurt

you?'

Through her tears she smiled, 'I have never been so happy, these are tears of joy'

Francis leant over to kiss the tears away. She reached out her hand and brushed her fingers against his body, moving lower until she was holding his penis in her hand. As he became aroused once more she stroked it and then bent over and took him in her mouth. When Francis could stand it no longer he pulled her on top of her and entered her again. He moved himself up and down slowly and she shuddered in delight. This time he took a long time to climax and when they had finished they lay close together his arms around her and fell asleep.

Francis awoke with a start not realising where he was and then he looked down at Kathryn asleep in his arms and he remembered smiling. Reality struck him and he remembered who they were. He was not sure how long they had been asleep but knew that they must hurry back to the Hall before they were missed. He woke Kathryn up.

'Quickly, it is getting late and they will wonder where we have been,' he said. 'I have so much I want to say to you but we have no time, you must get dressed.' Kathryn understood and put her clothes on and rearranged her hair. They brushed the leaves and dust from their clothes and set out for home. At the edge of the wood Francis took her in his arms and kissed her tenderly.

'I love you Kathryn,' he said. 'I only wish we had more time but I must take you back to your husband.'

'I love you too,' she replied. 'I will count the hours until I can see you again'. They then crossed the fields to the lane and walked quickly back. It was not as late as they feared and Kathryn had not been missed. Francis walked with her to the door of the house and they said their farewells. In a loud voice Kathryn said,

'Thank you for my lesson, I shall expect to see you to tomorrow at the same time'. She added softly, 'until then, my love'.

'It has been my pleasure Lady Kathryn,' Francis replied, and she understood his meaning from the look he gave her. Francis turned away from her and set off to walk back to the village.

As he walked back his heart was soaring and he relived every moment of their encounter but as he reached the village his mood became sombre as he thought of the sin they had just committed. He tried to push these thoughts away but his years of indoctrination by the church were not easy to push to one side, and by the time he reached his uncle's house he was filled with despair.

He entered the house and went to the small room where he slept. He threw himself on his bed clutching the cross about his neck and wept the tears streaming down his face. After some moments had passed his tears abated and with them his self pity; he rose from the bed and fell to his knees still clutching the cross and prayed for guidance.

It was some hours later when he heard his uncle calling for him that supper was on the table. Deep in prayer, Francis had not noticed the shadows lengthening. It was quite dark when he stood up and went out to his uncle and supper.

'There you are Francis, I have been looking for you for ages, the stew will be cold if we don't eat soon' said Father Wodewarde. Francis sat down at the table, tore a hunk of bread from the loaf of bread and ate his bowl of stew. 'Did you have a good day Francis?' Henry continued. 'I have not seen you since early morning prayers. You seem to have found your calling with your teaching.'

'Yes, uncle, it seems that I am a good teacher,' Francis said listlessly.

'Maybe that is what you should do when you return to your monastery; you have said often enough that you were unsure as to where your future lies,' said Henry, unaware of the turmoil in his nephew's mind.

'Uncle' - Francis started but could not continue and Henry looked up from his meal and saw for the first time the anguish and pain in Francis's face and said.

'But what is wrong Francis, you look so troubled, can I help?'

Francis wanted to tell his uncle but he couldn't bring himself to do so and he didn't want to lose the respect and pride which he knew Henry had for him, and so he tried to smile and said,

'Oh it is probably nothing, I am just a little tired that is all, I will finish my meal and have an early night if you don't mind.'

'If you are sure there is nothing wrong, you know that I am always here and willing to listen,' Henry said.

'No, I shall be fine after a good nights rest,' and Francis left the table and went back to his room to spend a restless night tossing and turning. When he did finally fall asleep he dreamt of Kathryn.

Chapter 17

When Francis left her, Kathryn had gone to her room. She sat in a chair, her thoughts dwelling on Francis and his love for her. Unlike him she was not feeling guilty or worrying that she had betrayed her husband. She was in love and her mind was full of the pleasure that they had found in each other's arms, and she eagerly looked forward to their next encounter. She lay there day dreaming until she saw that the room was getting dark. She got out of the chair, smoothed down her dress and tidied her hair and left her room. As she reached the top of the stairs she met her husband who had just ridden back from Kilborough. He was still untidy and dusty from his long ride. They exchanged greetings and he said that he was going to clean himself up and he would see her at dinner. Kathryn went downstairs in search of Viola and Thomas went to his room.

Viola was sitting with her daughter Margaret in the large hall. Viola, her hands always busy, had her embroidery on her lap and she was listening to her daughter who was relating her morning's work with Francis in the village. She invited Kathryn to sit at her feet on a small stool and a servant brought them all a glass of wine.

'Brother Francis is so good with the children, Mother,' Margaret was saying. 'This morning they were learning the letters of the alphabet and he brings the letters to life. Each child sits there listening to his every word and he had them all reciting the alphabet by the end of the morning. I am not sure that I will ever be as good with them.'

'Have you done any teaching yet?' her mother asked.

'No, but he suggests that I start with some of the younger girls and teach them to count.' Margaret answered, her face shining with enthusiasm. 'Do you find him to be a good teacher Kathryn?'

'Yes, in these last few weeks I have learnt so much; he is opening up the world for me.' Kathryn replied, eager to talk about Francis. 'He is very pleased with my progress and says that I'm an excellent pupil, but I think it is because he is such a good teacher.'

'I would agree with him, you are as quick a learner as I have found,' interrupted Viola. 'I never would have thought that the shy young bride that Thomas brought here a year ago could turn into such a capable housekeeper.' She looked at her daughter-in-law with affection. 'It seems that you are a scholar too.'

'You must come and see what we are doing,' said Margaret. 'I am sure Brother Francis's calling was to be a teacher.' They continued to chat idly and when Thomas came down the stairs they went through to sit at the table.

The conversation at the table was mainly about Thomas's trip to town and the business he had there.

'I met with your father,' he said to his wife. 'I invited then to stay as you requested and he thanked me and he hopes that they will be able to come for a few days next week. He will send a messenger to confirm it.'

'That is wonderful news.' Kathryn was delighted but then she realised it would mean she wouldn't be able to see Francis while they were here and her heart sank.

'Your younger sister and brother will also accompany them so you will have to keep them entertained.' Thomas said.

'Kathryn can organise the whole visit, it will be good experience for her,' Viola joined in. 'I will be there for guidance if you need it my dear,' she said to Kathryn.

'It is the village fair next week,' said Margaret.

'I had forgotten about that, you will be able to take your brother and sister,' said Viola.

'I was not here last year for the fair, I shall look forward to it.' Kathryn answered. 'Is it a very big one?'

'No, I am sure you will find it quite small in comparison to Kilborough fair,' explained Viola. 'It is held in the Churchyard and lasts for only two days. They come in from the surrounding villages to sell their produce and there are travelling sellers who visit. There is also entertainment; last year we had a stilt walker and acrobats. It is a chance for the villagers to enjoy themselves.'

'You enjoy it too mother,' said Thomas light-heartedly. He was in a good mood having spent the day with his friends in Kilborough.

'I admit that I do; it is useful to purchase things that are not normally available without visiting the town,' his mother replied. They continued to tell Kathryn about the fair as they finished their meal and when it was over, Thomas retired to his study and the ladies went to bed.

The next morning Kathryn was up early as she was eager to start on the arrangements for her parent's visit. Her first task was to organise the sleeping arrangements. There was only spare room for visitors and she considered asking Viola and Margaret to share. She decided that this wouldn't be fair as they were her relations and she sighed when she realised she must ask her husband to share her room.

Thomas had moved out his first wife's bed early in their marriage as she was so sickly and he had since grown used to sleeping on his own. When he had married Kathryn he had continued to sleep in his own room and Kathryn had been grateful for this. Her brother and sister, Edmund and Matilda would need to sleep somewhere and it would look odd if she suggested Matilda share with her and Thomas could hardly sleep with Edmund.

She went in search of her husband and she found him talking to Roger Tyler the bailiff by the stables as he was waiting for his horse to be saddled. He heard her as she approached and dismissed the bailiff and said to her,

'We have had news from your father; they will be coming to stay next week'.

'I am pleased,' she replied, 'I came to speak to you about their visit. Would you mind sleeping in my room during their visit so that Edmund and Matilda can have your bed?'

'But of course I don't mind, these past few weeks I have been considering moving back with you permanently. I have started to enjoy my nights with you.'

'You are too kind,' she said. 'If they are to be here next week I have much to do,' and she made her excuses and left her husband. She was trembling as she returned to the house and her eyes were filling with tears. She did not want him in her bed every night, she would rather he wasn't there at all. She wanted Francis.

The rest of the morning flew by; Kathryn was so busy she forgot all about Francis until a servant came to tell her he was waiting in the solar. She did not want him to wait while she changed her dress so she went to meet him as she was.

After an agonising night Francis had decided that he must tell Kathryn that what they had done was wrong and must never happen again. He would explain to her how important it was to him to be a monk and how important her marriage vows should be to her. He was full of good intentions but when Kathryn opened the door and entered the room her face flushed and her eyes sparkling he forgot all about them. His heart soared at the sight of her and he realised that he could never giver her up. She closed the door and flew into his arms; he held her and breathed in her smell wondering how he could ever imagine he could give her up. He lifted her face to his and kissed her on the lips and then he gently released her.

'We must be careful, someone might come in,' he said.

'They never have before,' she said.

'But we had nothing to hide then,' he answered.

'You are right, we must sit down,' she said, and went to sit in a chair. He did likewise, choosing one as close to her as he could; he rested his hand on her knee.

'We must talk Kathryn,' he said. 'I have spent all night thinking of you'.

'And I you.'

'I have not only thought about you and what we did yesterday, but also of the implications. What we did was a sin against God, your husband and everything that we have been taught.' She tried to interrupt but he took hold of both her hands and continued. 'Let me finish what I want to say. When I left here all I could think about was the wondrous gift that you gave me yesterday in the woods and how much I loved you. But I also love the Lord and have taken a vow of chastity and this is what I agonised over all night. This morning I made a decision, I was coming to tell you I could no longer give you lessons and that we must never meet alone again.'

Kathryn cried softly.

'No, I could not bear it.'

'That is what I had decided to tell you but as soon as you walked through that door I knew I could not go through with it. I could not live with the thought that I would never touch you or make love to you again. I don't know how this will end but even if we only have this summer I want to spend as much time as I can with you Kathryn. I love you and my love for you now is stronger than my devotion to God.' He finished speaking, his voice breaking with emotion. Kathryn stood up and buried her face in his lap and then raised her face and said,

'Yesterday was the happiest day of my life and I want us to repeat it. I now understand what they mean when they say you are making love. I never realised that the act of procreation could be so beautiful until you it has only brought me pain. I know of the risks that we are taking but if we are careful no one will find out and you my love are worth the risk.' Francis leant over and kissed her again and then he said.

'If we are going to be careful I suggest you sit on that chair and we start our lesson.'

Reluctantly Kathryn did so and they spent the next hour working on her French vocabulary touching and kissing whenever possible. She asked him if he would like a drink and she went to the kitchen to fetch some ale. When she returned she closed the door and turned the key in the lock and whispered,

'There is only the cook and one servant in the house, we will not be disturbed.' She placed the jugs of ale on the floor and walked over to where Francis was sitting. She pulled up his habit and found him ready for her.

'We must be quick Francis but I could not bear to wait any longer'

She sat astride him pushing her skirts to one side and he entered her with ease. They moved up and down on the chair in unison her arms around his neck, his around her waist. Kathryn climaxed quickly and he soon followed. She eased herself from him and they both made themselves look respectable. Kathryn walked on unsteady feet to the door, unlocked it and picked up the ale and returned to Francis and gave him one.

'I can't believe I just did that, you must think me very wanton,' she said. 'I have never acted like this before in my life.'

'I am glad you did,' Francis said, the colour of his face slowly returning to normal. 'I have wanted to make love to you all afternoon but did not dare suggest it. No, you are not wanton; you are still my sweet shy Kathryn.'

Kathryn laughed at this, spilling ale down her dress.

'I was worried I may not see you alone for some time as my family are to come and visit next week. I am looking forward to seeing them but I can't bear the thought that we will be apart. We are going to invite your uncle and you to dinner when they are here and my mother-in-law suggested that I go to the village fair with Edmund and Matilda, but it is not the same.'

'On one of your normal lesson days we could take your siblings out for a walk. It would help to establish a routine and when they have gone home we could continue to have one lesson a week outdoors,' he suggested.

'What a good idea,' she said. 'You will like Edmund and Matilda. Edmund is now sixteen and helps my father with his business; he is very studious but has a lively sense of humour. Matilda is twelve and in some ways she is still a child but she is turning into a beautiful young woman and likes to flirt at every opportunity.'

'Just like her sister,' Francis said jokingly. 'I shall have to be careful with two of you.' Kathryn slapped at his hands playfully.

They resumed their lesson and at the end of the afternoon Francis kissed her goodbye and left her to walk home.

Chapter 18

Rissa looked at her watch and exclaimed,

'Have you seen the time granny? This morning has flown by. We must be on our way or the carpet fitters will be waiting.' She started to collect all the papers they had been looking at together.

'You have been a great help Rissa, these documents are making my project so much easier,' answered Mary Montague. 'I now have names for the 15th and 16th centuries and can try and link them to the 19th century.'

'Yes and you also have to find where the name changed from de Montagu to Montague. It is interesting that the name Thomas runs through the centuries isn't it?'

'Yes and also one or two other names as well, your grandfather was Francis and his father was Harold. Just leave it all there dear as you are in a hurry,' said Mary when she saw her granddaughter looking for somewhere to put the pile of documents she had in her hand. 'I will just get my bag and then we can go. I am looking forward to seeing your house.' They left the house and Mary locked up. There were still police cars in the lane and there was a policeman stationed at the door of the Shahs. Rissa managed to manoeuvre her car out of the lane with difficulty and they made the short journey to Brook House.

'I hope all those cars have left when I return Rissa,' said Mary. 'They are a nuisance and I am still very worried about Jackie, maybe I will find out what has happened when we get back.'

'It certainly seems strange the police taking her off like that. They must have good reason to but I can't imagine what. Oh good, we've beaten the carpet fitters,' said Rissa as she drove into the entrance to Brook House. She parked the car and they both got out; Rissa opened the boot and removed the picnic hamper she had brought and they entered the house. Rissa led the way into the kitchen and put the hamper down on the worktop. Mary hadn't been to the house since it was at the very early stage of building and she looked around the kitchen admiringly.

'This is a nice spacious room Rissa, it is light and airy and with lots of cupboard space. Are you going to have a large kitchen table?'

'Yes we are. It is on order and should be arriving soon. Shall I give you the guided tour while we are waiting and then we can have lunch in here out of the way of the fitters?' Her grandmother nodded her head eagerly and Rissa took her through to show her the rest of the house, When they were upstairs a van drew up and Rissa left Mary and went down to see the fitters. They seemed to know where everything went and said they would start at the top of the house and work down. Mary came downstairs and said,

'I like the way you have made use of the loft; you will have to make sure it does not get too full of clutter.'

'All Simon's climbing gear is a worry, I think I will have to ban it from the house and he can store it in the garage,' Rissa said laughingly.' Do you want to see the gardens or shall we have lunch first?'

'I think lunch sounds like an excellent idea,' said Mary. Rissa went out to the car and got two picnic chairs out of the boot. As she shut the boot door George Allen came round the side of the house.

'Hello Rissa, I thought I saw you and Mary inside,' he said. 'We are just going home for a bite to eat. The patio is coming on well and we should be on target if the weather holds.'

'The carpets are being fitted and I thought it would be a chance to show granny round,' said Rissa. Mary came out of the front door and greeted George.

'George, Rissa has just been showing me the house you seem to have done an excellent job. Rissa has been helping me this morning with my family tree. Will you tell Eileen for me that we have made a breakthrough and I would like to show her sometime?'

'Yes, I can do that,' he said. 'Anne James that archaeologist is coming round tonight to see the

164

work Eileen has done on ours, so maybe she will have something to show you as well'.

'I forgot to mention that to you Granny,' Rissa said to her grandmother, and then to George. 'It must be serious if Jake is introducing her to the family.'

'I don't know about that, she seems nice enough and Jake likes her; he never stops talking about her,' George said.

'You'll find it busy in the village when you go home,' continued Rissa. 'The police took Jackie Shah away for questioning this morning.'

George looked surprised.

'What would they do that for? She is such a nice girl, so quiet and shy. Mind you I know you mustn't speak ill of the dead but that husband of hers must have been a trial to live with. Anyway I must be off; maybe I'll see you later.' And he went to his truck and drove off. Mary and Rissa returned to the kitchen with the chairs and Rissa unpacked the picnic. Mrs White had packed the basket full of goodies. There were hardboiled eggs, chickens legs, a salad and white crusty rolls. There was also a thermos of coffee and two small lemon mousses. Mary and Rissa sat on the picnic chairs and ate the meal from the white china plates Mrs White had thoughtfully provided. When they had finished Rissa took her grandmother into the garden and they walked around looking at the work that had been done so far and Rissa explained how it was intended to look when it was finished.

'I think it is all going to look beautiful when it is finished dear,' said Mary. 'I shall look forward to when you invite me round in the summer for afternoon tea and we can sit on the patio. Do you have to stay here all afternoon?'

'Yes I have to stay until the fitters are finished. I have brought some paperwork from the office with me,' answered Rissa.

'Well in that case I shall leave you and walk back to the village,' said Mary.

'If you are sure, I could easily run you back.'

'It's not far and the exercise will do me good,' said Mary. She collected her bag, saying that she would see Rissa soon, and headed back home. Rissa went and cleared up the debris of the picnic and went to check on the carpet fitters.

Rissa stayed at the house until the carpet fitters had finished for the day. They had completed upstairs and said they would be back the next day to do the downstairs. Before she left Rissa went around the back to find George Allen who was in the process of clearing up the patio with his son Jake.

'George, would you let the carpet fitters in if I am not here tomorrow? she asked.

'Sure that won't be a problem, do they know what they are doing?' he answered.

'I think so, I will be over to check up on them at some time during the day but I need to be at the livery stables to make sure everything is prepared for when I am away on my honeymoon.'

'I'm sure they are managing, Jenny says that you have everything very organised up there.'

'I do hope so, they are all hard workers and Daddy has said he will keep an eye on things while I'm away,' said Rissa. 'I hope you have a nice evening, perhaps there will be another wedding in your family soon,' and she winked at Jake.

'Steady on Rissa, you're as bad as everyone else.' Jake said, trying to look indignant but failing.

'Well I'm not sure Eileen would be pleased to see her only son leave home but it can't be too soon for me, not only would he go but also his bike and smelly leathers,' said his father joining in the fun.

'But you would be in a house full of women with only you to nag dad,' Jake retorted.

'True. I hadn't thought of that,' said George, and they all laughed. Rissa said goodbye and they all left to go home.

George and Jake drove home in companionable silence and as soon as they reached the house, Jake leapt out of the truck and raced upstairs to the bathroom.

'It's serious,' said Eileen Allen to husband as he came into the kitchen. 'That is the first time that I have ever seen him run to the bathroom in all his

19 years.'

'He does seem taken with her,' said George. 'If she's the one I hope he will be as happy with her as I am with you,' and he put his arms around his wife's ample waist and gave her a big sloppy kiss.

'Give over with you George, I'm busy and a wash might be a good idea for you too,' Eileen said, laughing as she held her nose between her fingers. George went off to wash and change and Eileen continued to prepare the vegetables for supper.

The twins were watching television and Jenny was laying the table for the evening meal; she came through to the kitchen for some glasses.

'Something smells good mum, what is it?' she said. 'Do I need to put wine glasses out?'

'Yes, I thought a drop of wine would be nice this evening, there is a bottle of white in the fridge and a red opened on the sideboard. I have made a chicken casserole and we will have it with jacket potatoes and cabbage. I hope Anne eats meat, I never thought to ask,' Eileen said.

'Everyone likes your cooking mum and I am sure she will eat it. Don't worry about her, she is very friendly, you'll like her,' her daughter said.

'Your father liked her when he met her; it's just that Jake has never brought a girl home before.'

'Jake invited her because he thought you would find her helpful with your research not because he is about to pop the question, he's only known her less than a week.'

'We'll see,' said Eileen and continued with the preparations for the meal.

Jake spent along time in the shower and then went to his room to get dressed. He splashed himself with aftershave and dressed with unusual care in a pair of tight black jeans and new grey shirt. He wanted to impress Anne, for although he had only known her a short time he knew he was falling in love with her.

Chapter 19

Anne arrived at the Allen home just before 7 o' clock. She had not wanted to come on the bike and a colleague from work had kindly given her a lift. She too had taken care with her appearance, choosing from her wardrobe one of her more sober outfits, cream jeans and a brown tweed jacket. In her hands she carried a bunch of flowers and a bottle of wine. She also had her large bag over her shoulder in which she had placed some data that she thought might help Mrs Allen. She was slightly nervous about her visit, as she was unused to a large family, being an only child. She wanted to make a good impression on Mrs Allen as she was growing very fond of Jake and knew that his mother was very important to him. She walked up the steps to the front door and rang the bell.

Jenny answered the door and said,

'Hi Anne, do come in, Jake is still upstairs getting ready. He even had a shower, you are honoured!' She showed Anne through into the large sitting room, which was very homely with large comfortable sofas and chairs. George was already sitting in his favourite armchair but he stood up when Anne entered and went over to shake her hand.

'It's nice to see you again Anne, and in slightly better circumstances. Please sit down. Can I get you a drink, a beer or sherry maybe?'

'A glass of beer would be lovely and I have brought you this,' said Anne, handing over the wine.

'That is very kind of you,' he answered, and left the room to fetch her a drink. Anne heard the sound of footsteps running downstairs and moments later Jake came into the room.

'Oh Anne, it is good to see you,' and he swiftly made his way across the room to her and gave her a big hug and a kiss lifting her off her feet. Jenny coughed quietly.

'Don't mind me,' she said. 'I'll just go and see if mum wants any help' and she left the room.

'Would you please put me down,' said Anne. 'I am hardly going to impress your parents six inches off the ground.' He lowered her to the ground and led her to a sofa where they sat down and she let him put his arm around her. George came back in the room followed by his wife Eileen; Anne stood up and said

'Hello Mrs Allen, it was kind of you to invite me. I am looking forward to your cooking. Jake has told me what a wonderful cook you are. Oh I nearly forgot these are for you,' and she handed over the bunch of flowers.

'How lovely, Jake must have told you how fond of tulips I am. I hope my cooking meets your expectations. We will be eating in about fifteen minutes so you just sit down and enjoy your drink,' said Eileen and she went back to the kitchen. George gave Anne her beer and Jenny brought one in for Jake and they all sat down. The door burst open and Nicola and Sophie ran into the room. They looked at Jake sitting on the sofa close to Anne and giggled.

'You haven't met the youngest members of our family yet Anne, this is Nicola and Sophie,' said George.

'Trouble!' said Jake.

'Hello,' said Anne to the twins. 'You will have to tell me who is who'.

'I'm Nicola and this is Sophie,' declared Nicola. 'I am taller than Sophie but she has more freckles'.

'Nicola is also the noisier one,' said Jenny. 'They are identical and take great delight in confusing people but they don't often catch us out.' Nicola came over to Anne, closely followed by Sophie,

'Harry told us all about the skeleton that was found can we come and see it?' she asked.

'Yes you can if someone can bring you to the museum,' Anne replied.

'We found a body too,' said Sophie quietly. 'It was Mr Shah and he was covered in blood'.

'Yes, I know, it must have been awful for you' said Anne, sensing that Sophie was upset. 'Come and sit by me and I will tell you about the pilgrim that Rissa found.' Sophie climbed onto the sofa and sat beside Anne. Nicola came to sit on her other side wriggling her way in between Jake and Anne.

'Move over Jake,' she said. 'What is that smell?' She sniffed at her brother and turned to Anne 'he is smelling like that for you, you know he was in the bathroom for ages this evening.' Jake's face reddened and he dug Nicola in the ribs.

'You didn't have to tell her that,' he said. 'You are lucky having no sisters like these two little horrors'.

'Well I think you smell very nice,' said Anne and then to the two girls she said 'and he is also lucky to have you two.'

Every one settled down and Anne told the girls about the skeleton and they plied her with questions. Eileen came into the room and announced that dinner was ready and they all stood up.

'You are tiny, Anne,' said Sophie. 'I am nearly as tall as you, can I hold your hand?' and she took Anne's hand and they all went through to the dining room.

The twins both wanted to sit next to Anne and when Jake objected Nicola said,

'You can have her later.' Everyone laughed and Jake sighed and gave in, letting his sisters sit with Anne. Eileen served the casserole and told everyone to help themselves to vegetables. Jake poured the wine and they all started to eat.

'This is delicious,' exclaimed Anne. 'Jake was not

exaggerating; it makes a nice change from meals for one in my small flat.'

'Have you bought the flat or do you rent?' asked George.

'I am renting but if I stay in the area I would like to buy somewhere, probably a small cottage in one of the villages,' answered Anne.

'If you need any help you can always ask me and I am sure Jake would help with any renovations,' said George.

'That's kind of you but I haven't started looking yet.'

'When you marry Jake you could come and live in Chadsbury Green,' said Sophie.

'It's a bit soon for that Sophie, we've only just met,' Jake said.

'But we would like you to marry Anne and then she would be our sister,' continued Sophie.

'And I could have your room,' countered Nicola.

'You seem to be a hit Anne,' said Eileen. 'Eat up everyone and I will fetch the pudding. Jenny cleared the dishes and Eileen brought in a large gooseberry pie and a big jug of custard and they all tucked in. When the meal was finished Eileen suggested they clear the table and she could show Anne her research into the Allen family tree. She went to fetch her file and laid everything out on the dining room table.

'I have concentrated on the Allen family, not my

own which comes from a nearby village. We know that the family has been in the village for generations, you can tell by looking at the gravestones in the churchyard. This house is three hundred years old and as far as we can tell there has always been an Allen living in it,' reported Eileen.

'You seem to have done a lot of work,' said Anne, studying the tree laid out in front of her. 'I like the way you have also noted the employment of each generation. I see that they have been in the building trade in some form or another for the last few hundred years. In my bag I have some old documents which may help you.'

'I'll get it,' said Nicola, and she went out of the room to fetch Anne's bag. 'Is this it?'

'Yes, thank you,' said Anne, reaching into the bag and removing a folder. 'Rissa also has a copy of this, which she gave to her grandmother. I looked up the name Allen and I found a family called Aleyn in the 17th century which is the early spelling of Allen.'

'I found that name and wondered if it was the same name. If it is then it will make my research so much easier,' said Eileen.

'I am sure you will find that it is the same family. You will find that originally they were just peasants working on the land but there were also a few generations when they were bailiffs to the de

Montagu family at Chadsbury Hall. Shall I leave these records with you to look at?'

'Yes please Anne you have been a great help,' answered Eileen.

'Sophie and Nicola would like to come to the museum to see the skeleton of the pilgrim, perhaps you could bring them on Saturday morning and you may also find the museum of interest,' Anne said.

'That sounds like a good idea and I could bring Mary Montagu,' replied Eileen standing up and looking at the twins. 'If you will excuse me but these two need to go to bed.'

'Not yet,' they chorused.

'Now!' said their father.

'I'll come and say goodnight if you would like,' said Anne. The girls nodded and went up to bed closely followed by Mrs Alan.

'They are good girls really but hard work,' said George. 'I don't remember Jake and the others being such a handful - maybe it's because I am getting older'.

'It must have been hard work bringing up seven of them,' Anne said. 'I'm an only child. Is Sophie troubled by finding the body? I notice she seems very quiet in comparison to her sister.'

'She has had nightmares the last two nights and mum has had to sit with her.' Jenny said. 'Mum is also worried about Nicola who is more boisterous than usual. She is thinking of taking them both to

176

trauma counselling if things don't improve. Dad, do you know if they have found who did it yet?'

'Rissa said today that they have taken Jackie Shah in for questioning but I don't know anymore.' he replied.

'I can't imagine Jackie harming a fly.' said Jake. 'Why don't we all go up to the Angel and find out the latest?'

'Yes, do that dad, and take mum; I'll stay with the twins,' said Jenny. Eileen came back downstairs and said,

'If you don't mind Anne, they are ready for you to go and say goodnight'.

'I'll show her up,' offered Jake and he took her up to say goodnight.

'Mum, I suggested that you all went to the Angel to see if there is any more news about Dezi Shah,' said Jenny.

'I would rather not leave Sophie, but you and dad go if you want,' Eileen said tiredly.

'No, I will stay in with you tonight love,' said George.

'I will too,' said Jenny.

Jake and Anne came downstairs and Jake said,

'Is anyone going to the pub?'

'Not tonight Jake,' his father said.

'Anne didn't come on her bike so I will need to run her back in the car if that's alright dad?'

'Would you like some coffee before you go

Anne?' asked Eileen.

Anne looked at Jake who shook his head and so she said,

'No thank you, I have enjoyed myself this evening and you must let me know how you get on with the Allen family.'

'It's been our pleasure, you must come again and I will see you on Saturday,' said Eileen.

'I look forward to it,' replied Anne, and she and Jake left the house.

'Do you want to go to the Angel?' Jake enquired

'Only if you do,' said Anne. 'I would prefer to go home, we can be alone there.'

'That sounds like a far better idea,' said Jake as he unlocked the car.

'I have enjoyed myself this evening, you have a nice family,' remarked Anne as she slid into the car. She leant over and kissed him on the cheek. Jake smiled and said

'I'll give you a proper kiss when we get to your flat,' and he turned the ignition and they set off for Kilborough.

Chapter 20

Kathryn woke up early to find her bedroom bathed in brilliant sunshine, she remembered that today was the day her parent's were coming to stay. She quietly crept out of bed so as not to disturb her husband who was still asleep. He had moved into her room two days before but she had feigned sleep when he came to bed and he had not bothered her. She dressed and stole out of the room and ran downstairs to the kitchen. She poured herself some cider and sat down at the table to study her list of things to do for her parent's visit.

Since the visit had been confirmed she had been very busy; her lessons with Francis had been cancelled and she had not seen him. Tonight he was coming with his uncle to dine with them and she had prepared a special meal in honour of her family's visit. They were to eat venison and swan and Viola had shown Kathryn how to make her special junket for pudding. She was up so early that no one else was about and it was fifteen minutes before the cook appeared in the kitchen. She was surprised to see Kathryn there so early but said good morning and went about her business preparing a meal for the household when they rose. She assured her young mistress that everything was in control in the kitchen for the evening's banquet and breathed a sigh or relief when Kathryn left the kitchen.

Kathryn went out to the dairy to check on the junket she had made the day before. She collected a basket and stepped out to the kitchen garden to pick gooseberries to go with the milk pudding. Viola had created the kitchen garden when she had arrived at the Hall as a young bride. Kathryn found that like her mother-in-law she too enjoyed working in the garden. She filled her basket with gooseberries and then sat on a small stool enjoying the sunshine before returning with them to be washed in the kitchen.

The rest of her morning sped by as she checked that the bedrooms were ready and all her other preparations were in place. Finally she admitted to herself that everything was in order and she returned to sit by the window of her bedroom and watch for the arrival of her family.

At about two o'clock she saw them riding up the drive towards the house and she raced down the stairs to greet them. Her father was driving her mother and sister in a small cart but her brother had ridden over on a horse along with two servants who were there for protection against footpads. Kathryn ran out of the house to meet them and was treated to a large hug from her brother who had just dismounted.

'Hullo Edmund, you seem taller than when I last saw you,' Kathryn said as she returned his embrace and then she went over to her mother and father.

'Oh I have missed you so,' she said tearfully and went into her mothers arms while her father looked at her fondly.

'We miss you too,' he said. 'It was kind of your husband to allow us to visit you here'.

'Yes it was,' Kathryn said. 'He can sometimes be kind.' She then looked at her younger sister. 'Matilda, you too have grown so, I hardly recognised you, you are quite the young lady.'

In answer Matilda spun in a circle and curtsied to her sister.

'I can assure you her manners are not always that pretty, she is still a terror,' Kathryn's mother said. 'You are looking well Kathryn; you seem livelier than when we last saw you. Are you settling in at last?'

'Yes, mother I am much more content, but where are my manners, you must come inside and I will fetch you something to eat and drink. You must be tired after your long journey.'

They made there way into the house and Kathryn showed them into the solar and left them there while she went in search of some refreshments. She returned with a servant carrying a tray of cordial, ale, bread, cheese and ham.

'I trust this will be sufficient until we eat this evening. We are to have a small banquet in your honour and the priest and his nephew will be coming. Francis the nephew has been spending time

181

with me at my lessons as my husband felt I lacked an education.'

'You can read and write?' enquired her mother, puzzled.

'Ah, but Lord de Montagu is a scholar my dear' said her husband. 'Kathryn has only had a basic education. When I spoke to him last week he said how pleased he was with how Kathryn has progressed recently.'

'I have enjoyed it and I now understand a little Latin and can converse in French. Francis is a very good teacher. You must tell me your news, it has been so long since I have been to Kilborough,' said Kathryn.

They spent the rest of the afternoon talking and reminiscing about old times and then Kathryn showed them to their rooms and left them to rest while she went to check on preparations for the evening meal.

Everyone was in the Great Hall when Henry and Francis Wodewarde arrived. Richard and Mary Leys had met the priest before but they did not know Francis and introductions were made. Matilda made her curtsey and fluttered her eyelashes at Francis. At twelve years old Matilda was just becoming aware that she was a woman and liked to practice her charms whenever she got the chance.

They all sat down and the servants brought the food in.

'This is excellent,' said Mary Leys to Viola. 'You have been very busy.'

Didn't Kathryn tell you she has made all the preparations for your visit including this meal? I am waiting to try her junket which she has made to my recipe,' said Viola.

'I'm impressed,' said Mary.' You never said, Kathryn how busy you had been'.

Kathryn blushed and said,

'Lady Viola has been teaching me and this week she has let me loose all on my own, I am sure I have been driving everyone mad but I wanted everything to be just right'.

'Cook did mention that you were looking over her shoulder all morning,' laughed Viola. 'I am very proud of what she has achieved and so must you be,' she said to the Leys.

'She is also becoming quite a scholar thanks to Brother Francis,' her husband added.

'Thank you sire,' said Kathryn 'and to you too,' she added, looking at Francis.

'Yes, Brother Francis is turning out to be quite a good teacher, he is even teaching some of the children in the village and my sister is helping,' said Thomas. 'We will all miss him when he returns to his monastery.'

'When do you return?' asked Richard Leys.

'I am due to return in the autumn but I am undecided as to my future,' replied Francis.

'I have been trying to persuade him to stay longer and help me,' said his uncle. The conversation continued around the table and everyone declared Kathryn's junket to be a success. At the end of the meal the men sat at the table to discuss politics. Margaret stayed with the men and Francis suggested that he and Edmund might play a game of chess. The two older women retired to the solar and Kathryn and her sister sat and watched the chess game. Francis was the better player and he won.

'That was a good game Edmund, we must play again,' he said. 'Would you like to come for a walk tomorrow afternoon we could take your sisters?'

'We would like that,' answered Edmund. 'Wouldn't we Matilda?'

'Yes we would,' said his younger sister.

Kathryn smiled at the way Francis had cleverly arranged the walk and added.

'We could visit the river and go fishing.'

'The day after tomorrow is the village fair; will you be bringing your family Lady Kathryn?' asked Francis innocently.

'I hope so,' said Matilda eagerly. 'I love the fair.'

'This one isn't as big as Kilborough but Lady Viola said we would all enjoy it so I am planning to take you there,' said Kathryn.

In the solar the two older ladies were talking about Kathryn.

'Kathryn seems so much happier, Lady Viola,' said Mary. 'I am so grateful to you.'

'Well, I must admit she didn't impress me when she first came here, but I thought it was only fair to give her a chance; I won't be here for ever and I'm glad I did,' said Viola. 'However her happiness is not all my doing, she also has her lessons with Brother Francis.'

'I noticed she seems to enjoy his company. Do you think they are too close?'

'You too have noticed? I am sure there is nothing to worry about but as her mother you may like to speak to her,' said Viola.

'I shall do that,' said Mary. 'If you will excuse me but I am very tired and I think I will retire for the night.'

Chapter 21

Kathryn spent the morning with her parents showing them round the Hall. Edmund had gone riding with Thomas and Matilda was playing in the garden with a kitten.

'You seem so happy, Kathryn,' said Richard. 'I am glad things are finally working out for you. I was very worried in the early days of your marriage and did wonder if I had done the right thing but your husband was such a good catch and he has a fine estate.'

'I admit I was homesick to begin with but now with my household duties and my lessons I am beginning to enjoy life in the country. Brother Francis has been a good friend and I have learnt so much from him.'

'And what of your husband?' asked Mary

'Thomas is a quiet man, but he is kind, and these last few weeks I have been more comfortable in his company.'

'Let's hope you give him an heir soon,' declared Mary. 'His first wife was a disappointment to him.'

'I too hope for children, mother,' said Kathryn, quietly thinking of Francis. 'What would you like to do today? I am going for a walk with Francis and the children we shall probably go to the river to fish.'

'I am spending the afternoon with your husband

looking at the estate,' replied Richard.

'I shall be quite happy to sit in the sun and do nothing,' said Mary. 'I don't often get the chance to be lazy at home. It is very kind of Brother Francis to go for a walk with you. Do you perhaps not spend too much time with him Kathryn?'

'Leave the child be Mary, Sir Thomas approves of the relationship so where is the harm?' her husband said.

'She is no longer a child but a married woman.'

'He is my teacher and also my friend mother. Thomas is almost the same age as father, Francis is nearer my own age and I like him,' Kathryn said, not looking at her mother.

'Brother Francis,' corrected her mother, and said no more.

Edmund returned from his ride with Thomas. He had been unsure of spending the morning with the older man but although they had not spoken much Thomas had treated him as an equal and listened when Edmund did say anything. He went in search of his sisters and found them in the solar.

'Is there anything to eat Kathryn I'm hungry after my ride?' he asked.

'We have already eaten but there is some soup and cold venison waiting for you. You must eat it quickly, as we will be going out for our walk soon,' Kathryn said. He left the room in search of sustenance and Kathryn continued talking to Matilda.

'I hope you are doing your chores at home and helping mother Matilda.'

'Yes I do, since you left I have had to take on yours as well. I don't mind but it is not as much fun as when you were there to help me,' answered Matilda. 'I also have my lessons but mother is very kind and allows me to visit with my friends.'

'What do you with your friends?'

'We play games, practise dancing and talk about boys'.

'Are there any boys that you are particularly interested in?' asked Kathryn remembering when she was the same age.

'There is one friend of Edmunds; his name is Harold, his father is the corn merchant. I like him and I think he likes me, but don't you dare tell Edmund.'

'I won't,' said Kathryn laughing.

'I don't want to marry someone like Sir Thomas, he is so old.'

'Promise me Matilda, if you have the opportunity marry someone who is young and who you love,' Kathryn said passionately. 'Grab your chance before it is too late.'

'Are you unhappy with Sir Thomas?' asked Matilda, looking at her sister with concern.

'No, my husband may be old but I am well provided for,' said Kathryn dully.

'It's a shame Brother Francis is a monk, he is

good looking and he likes you,' said Matilda teasing.

'He is a good friend Matilda, that is all,' said Kathryn, and the look that she gave her sister left Matilda in no doubt that the subject was closed.

They went to find Edmund who was just finishing his meal with Thomas.

'I hear you are going fishing,' said Thomas. 'Perhaps you will catch something to eat?'

'I doubt it,' said Kathryn. 'I hope you enjoy your afternoon with father; it is kind of you to spend some time with my family.'

'I enjoy your father's company and I had a good ride with Edmund this morning; we must have them to stay more often.' At that moment Francis entered the Hall.

'Good afternoon Sir Thomas,' he said.

'Greetings Brother Francis, you have come to amuse my wife and her young guests? Well, don't let me keep you, I must go and meet Richard at the stables,' said Thomas and he stood up and went out.

Francis greeted Kathryn and her brother and sister.

'Are you ready?'

'I think so, I just have to collect the fishing lines,' said Kathryn, and she went to find them.

'Have you had a good morning?' asked Francis of the two younger ones.

'Yes sir, I had a good ride with Sir Thomas,' answered Edmund.

'I have been playing with a kitten,' said Matilda shyly.

Kathryn returned and they set off for the river. Francis and Edmund walked on ahead and the two sisters followed them stopping every so often to smell the flowers in the hedgerows. Francis and Edmund reached the river and waited for Kathryn and Matilda.

'Do you not find that you always have to wait for the women?' said Edmund.

'I don't have much experience with women,' said Francis wryly.

'Of course you don't,' replied Edmund. 'I forgot, you seem so normal,' he realised what he said and stood there looking embarrassed. 'I am sorry, I did not mean anything by that, it's just that I can't imagine what your life is like.'

Francis just laughed.

'Don't worry about it. My life is not so bad. My boyhood in the monastery was very happy and since then I have seen some of the world, which is more than most men manage.'

'I would love to travel but so far I have only been on some business trips to Norfolk with my father. What were France and Spain like? Do you not find Chadsbury Green quiet after your travels?'

'France and Spain are very similar to here only they speak a different language and it is hotter. As to Chadsbury Green I am finding my stay here very different to what I imagined. I have my work in the village and of course I spend time with your sister; she is a very unusual woman.'

'Kathryn and I have always been close and I missed her when she got married. I was very upset to hear she was unhappy but now I am pleased she has found a friend in you,' Edmund said. 'Hurry up you two,' he shouted to his sisters.

They positioned themselves on the riverbank and settled down to fish, Edmund and Kathryn laughing at Francis's attempts to show Matilda the correct way to cast a line. They stood there in silence for some time until there was a loud shout from Matilda.

'I think I've caught one!' Francis went to help her pull in the fish - it was a small river trout. Edmund caught another one soon after but Kathryn and Francis had no luck.

'We shall try further up the river,' said Kathryn to her brother and sister, but they did not really notice when the two lovers crept away.

Kathryn and Francis walked quickly up the river until they were out of sight of the two younger ones and fell into each other's arms. Francis kissed Kathryn passionately and pulled her down to the ground. They lay beside the river entwined, their hands and lips moving urgently over each other's bodies, but finally Kathryn disengaged herself and sat up.

'We must not stay here too long or they will worry, but I wanted to feel your kisses Francis, it has been so long.'

'For me too my love,' responded Francis. He stood up and set up their fishing lines saying, 'Maybe we will catch some fish,' and he returned to sit beside her and held her hand, stroking it as he did so. They stayed like that for quite some time not speaking just kissing and caressing and then with a sigh Kathryn spoke.

'We must go back,' she whispered, and they reluctantly stood up and returned to the children. While they had been sitting there both of their lines had caught a fish and they showed these to Edmund and Matilda.

'We have caught far more than you,' said Matilda scornfully. 'I have three and Edmund has five.'

'We will be able to eat them this evening,' said Kathryn.

'Francis must take two home for his supper with his uncle,' announced Matilda. 'He can have your two.'

'You are so kind Madam,' said Francis teasingly. 'If you have finished fishing I know of a place downstream where we can paddle our feet.'

'Yes please,' she said. 'I am hot,' and they collected their fishing tackle, put the fish in the basket that Kathryn had brought and followed Francis to a place where they could cross the river by stepping-stones.

They all sat down on the riverbank and removed their shoes or sandals and paddled in the water. Matilda laughed at the sight of Francis lifting up his skirts to keep them from the water.

'You do look odd,' she said. 'Are you not hot in that habit?'

'Matilda, don't be rude,' remonstrated her brother. 'Brother Francis looks no funnier than you do. I am the only one not hampered by skirts,' and to prove this he crossed the river nimbly jumping from one stone to another. Matilda not to be outdone went to follow her brother, tripped and fell into the river. It was not deep and she did not hurt herself but she was wet through. Edmund on the other side of the river laughed at the sight of his drenched sister and Kathryn and Francis joined in. Matilda burst into tears.

'Don't cry, Matilda,' said Kathryn, helping her sister out of the river. 'We will soon get you home and into some dry clothes. We are sorry we laughed but you do look funny.'

The younger girl continued to sniff crying and said crossly,

'I wish I was a boy and then I wouldn't have to wear skirts.'

'You are too pretty to be a boy,' said Francis, gently trying to placate her.

She stopped crying and answered him.

'I wish you were not a monk and then I could marry you.' Francis did not reply.

'Edmund, come back here and we will go home,' shouted Kathryn.

Edmund returned to their side of the river and they walked briskly back to the house.

They did not notice William Aleyn watching them from the other side of the river. He had been there for quite some time spying on them. He had watched Francis and Kathryn walking back to the children along the riverbank and their antics by the stepping stones.

'Interesting,' he thought, and crept away unseen.

Chapter 22

Matilda suffered no ill effects from her ducking apart from her pride. The family had eaten the trout with their evening meal and Edmund had regaled the company with the story of his sister's exploits, much to Matilda's mortification. She was cheered up when Lady Viola reminded her that they would visit the village fair the next day.

Late the next morning the party set off for the village. Sir Thomas said that he had things to do but he might join them later, and it was agreed that Richard would take his wife and Lady Viola in the cart. Lady Margaret said that she would walk there with Kathryn and her brother and sister, and they left earlier than the older members of the party. Lady Margaret was in a good mood and she answered Matilda and Edmund readily when they plied her with questions about the fair.

'I have visited the fair every year since I can remember,' she said. 'My mother brought me even when I was a little girl and I remember I was very scared by the stilt-walkers who looked so big. Since then I have been to Kilborough Fair many times but I still enjoy our small one'.

'You have lived here along time, have you never wanted to live anywhere else with a husband and a family?' asked Matilda.

'When I was your age I had dreams like any

young girl, but no handsome stranger ever came to sweep me off my feet and now I am too old,' she answered bitterly. 'But I am content now with my life. I have my books and horses, and I help to care for the sick. Recently Brother Francis has asked me to help with his school so I imagine I shall spend the rest of my days here if Kathryn and my brother do not turn me out.'

'We would never do that,' exclaimed Kathryn. 'Whatever gave you that idea?'

'I haven't exactly been friendly to you since you came here. I should have spent more time with you, helped you to settle in.'

'It doesn't matter,' said Kathryn taking hold of Margaret's hand. 'As long as we are friends now.'

'Of course we are,' said Margaret gruffly, but she did not remove her hand.

'We must be getting near the village, I can hear music,' said Edmund, and he took hold of Matilda's hand and they raced towards the village with Margaret and Kathryn following at a more sedate pace.

The fair was held in the churchyard and as they neared it they could see stalls and throngs of people.

'I must go and visit Mistress Dove, Kathryn, I will join you later,' said Margaret and she continued through the village. Kathryn caught up with her brother and sister and they stood on the edge of

the churchyard surveying the sights and sounds of
the fair. Villagers curtseyed or bowed to Kathryn as
they passed and she bid those she knew good day.
There were wondrous smells wafting across from
the food sellers who were selling pies, ale and nuts.

'I'm hungry,' declared Edmund.

'Here is some money,' said Kathryn. 'Go and
buy us a herring pie and we will wait for you here.'
He went of in search of the pie seller and Kathryn
and Matilda sat on a fallen log content to watch the
crowds of people.

'Good day, Lady Kathryn and Matilda, I trust
you have recovered from your soaking?' said
Francis who appeared beside them. 'Have you been
here long?'

'I am dry now and we are waiting for Edmund
who has gone to buy us a pie,' replied Matilda.

'We have not been here long, and soon our parents and Lady Viola should be here,' added
Kathryn

'I see Edmund returning with your pie so I will
leave you to eat it and perhaps I will see you later,'
and he left them greeting Edmund as he passed
him. Edmund distributed the pie and they ate it; it
was delicious. As they finished eating it the cart
arrived and Richard Leys called to them.

'It didn't take you long to find the food,
Edmund,' he said. 'What is it you are eating?'

'Herring pie,' Edmund said. 'Would you like me

to fetch some more, I am still hungry'.

Richard conferred with the ladies and they said they would like some pie. Richard stepped down from the cart, tethered the horse and went with Edmund to buy some more pies and cider to drink. Kathryn and Matilda went and sat in the cart with Viola and Mary.

'Have you had a look around yet?' asked Viola.

'No, not yet, Edmund insisted on eating,' said Kathryn.

'He never stops,' said his mother. Edmund and Richard returned with the refreshments. Kathryn and Matilda didn't want anymore pie but they each drank some cider.

'Can we go now?' asked Matilda.

'Yes, you go off with Edmund and Kathryn and we will follow shortly,' said Viola.

'Take this, you may need it, and watch for pickpockets,' said Richard, and handed over some pennies to Kathryn.

'Thank you, father,' she said, and then with her siblings she went into the churchyard.

Edmund held both his sisters' hands as he made his way through the crowds. They reached the stalls, stopped and looked around.

'What do you want to see?' he asked.

'Everything,' declared Matilda.

'Shall we walk down here and see what they are selling?' suggested Kathryn and they walked down an avenue of stalls stopping every so often to look at something of interest. There were stalls selling local produce such as pigeons, hens and honey. There was also the salt man, a malt seller and many other traders. The noise made by the crowds and the traders was deafening.

Kathryn and Matilda shouted at Edmund that they wanted to stop and look at a peddler's tray. The peddler had an assortment of combs for the hair, and they chose one each. As Kathryn reached for her purse, it was snatched from her hand and she was pushed to the ground.

'Stop thief!' shouted Edmund and he chased after the pickpocket. The thief weaved in and out through the throng of people with Edmund close on his heels shouting for someone to stop him. The thief reached the edge of the crowd to find his path blocked by the large figure of Edward Smithson, the blacksmith who grabbed hold of him and threw him to the ground and then he sat on him. Edmund arrived shortly after panting with his exertions.

'Well done, I thought I was going to lose him. He has just taken my sister's purse.'

'I am glad to be of help, sir,' said Edward. 'Is this what he stole?' And he showed Edmund the purse which he had removed from the thief's hand.

'Yes, that is Kathryn's,' said Edmund, who was slowly recovering his breath. 'What shall we do with him?'

'We need to find the sheriff's men, they can deal with him. The Sheriff of Kilborough usually sends two of his men over to the fair, as there is nearly always trouble.' Edward saw Robert Aleyn in the crowd and called him over. 'Robert, can you fetch the sheriff's men? I can't be sitting on top of this villain all day.' Robert hurried off and soon returned with two men in the livery of the sheriff. Edward explained what had happened.

'We'll take him back with us to Kilborough,' said one of the men. 'There will be a trial and we will need a witness.'

'My name is Edmund Leys,' said Edmund. 'I live in Kilborough and it was my sister's purse that this man stole. I saw it all.' The sheriff's men said they would be in touch, Edward released the thief and they hauled him off.

'I don't know your name,' said Edmund, shaking Edwards's hand. 'My sister is Lady Kathryn de Montagu, and I would like to thank you.'

'I am Edward Smithson and I know Lady Kathryn. I am the village blacksmith. I will walk back with you and we can see if she is alright'.

They walked back through the crowd to find Kathryn. They found her sitting on the ground, looking shaken. Kneeling over her was Francis his face full of concern. He looked up as Edmund and Edward appeared.

'Edmund, I think your sister hurt her ankle

when she fell to the ground; I have sent Matilda to find Lady Margaret. Perhaps you could help me carry her back to your parents' cart?'

'I can take her if you can show me where the cart is,' said Edward, and he gently lifted Kathryn in his strong arms and followed Edmund and Francis to the cart. When they reached the cart there was no sign of anyone. Edward laid Kathryn down and said,

'I hope your injury is not too serious, Lady Kathryn. I must leave now as I have work to do at the forge. Today is a busy day for me.'

'Thank you Edward,' said Kathryn weakly.

'Yes we all thank you, you must buy yourself a drink on me,' said Edmund, and he gave him a silver penny. Edward accepted the money from the young man and went back to his forge.

'I will go and see where Matilda and Lady Margaret are,' said Edmund.

'That's a good idea, I don't know what's keeping them,' said Francis and he gave him directions to Mistress Dove's. When Edmund had left, Francis whispered to Kathryn.

'I was jealous of Edward Smithson when he took you in his arms and carried you, I wanted it to be me.'

'But it wouldn't have looked seemly and you were there to look after me,' she said, wincing in pain as she did so.

'Does it hurt, my love?'

'A little,' she replied, and then she saw Edmund returning with Margaret. 'It looks like help is at hand'.

'Edmund and Matilda have told me what has happened,' said Margaret arriving at the cart. 'I am sorry we took so long but I needed to bring some ointments and bandages with me,' and she gently removed Kathryn's sandal and looked at her swollen ankle. 'I think it is only sprained Kathryn, it will be badly bruised and you will need to rest it for a few days. I will rub this salve in; it is made from comfrey and marsh mallow and should help the bruising.'

'It feels better already,' said Kathryn as Margaret applied the salve.

'Will you be alright now?' asked Matilda. 'I was very worried.'

'I am sure she will be,' answered Margaret, we just need to get her home to rest'.

'I can see your parents and Lady Viola coming over,' said Francis. 'Your father seems to be laden down with parcels.'

'Kathryn, we have just heard about your escapade and we came as quick as we could,' said her mother.

'I am fine mother, Lady Margaret assures me my ankle is only sprained and will soon be better.'

'I hear that you were quite the hero, son, catching the thief,' said Richard Leys.

'I had a little help from the blacksmith,' Edmund said.

'If you mean Edward Smithson I am not surprised the thief was stopped, Edward is very large and strong,' said Viola.

'I was scared when Edmund ran after the thief and left me alone with Kathryn but then Francis came and took charge,' Matilda said.

'She was very brave and went to find Lady Margaret,' added Francis.

'Kathryn is looking tired, we must get her home,' said her mother.

'You don't all have to come,' answered Kathryn. 'There is still so much to see and I don't want to spoil your day.'

'I am quite tired and ready to return home,' said Viola.

'So am I,' agreed Mary Leys.

'They certainly have bought plenty,' said Richard. 'I had to carry it.'

'Why don't I drive the cart home with Kathryn, Mary and mother and the rest of you can stay here and enjoy yourselves,' suggested Margaret.

'Do that,' said Kathryn, and it was agreed. Viola and Mary sat in the cart with Kathryn and they set off home.

'You must tell me what you bought,' said Kathryn to the two older women as they rode in the cart.

'There was so much good local produce,' said Mary. 'It is much fresher here than in Kilborough and Viola knew many of the local sellers. Amongst other things I bought some honey, duck eggs and some cheese which Viola has assured me will be excellent'.

'It may not be a big fair,' said Viola, 'but the quality is excellent. I too bought some honey and I also bought some embroidery silks and a pair of gloves, we enjoyed ourselves didn't we Mary?'

'Yes we did, it was nice to have someone to walk around with. I think Richard may enjoy himself more now without us,' and Mary laughed.

'Your poor father just followed us around and took our parcels as we handed them to him,' Viola stopped talking as she felt the cart slowing down. 'Why are we stopping Margaret?'

'I can see Thomas riding towards us,' said her daughter. Thomas slowed his horse down when he neared the cart and said,

'You are going back so soon? I was just coming to join you.' He noticed his wife lying in the back looking very pale. 'Is Kathryn not well?'

'Her purse was stolen and the thief pushed her to the ground as he grabbed it,' said Margaret. 'She has hurt her ankle but I don't think it is too serious.'

Thomas dismounted and came closer to the cart to speak to his wife.

'Are you in pain my dear? Did they catch the man who did this?' he said, anger in his voice.

'I just need to rest Thomas and yes, Edmund and Edward Smithson caught the thief. I believe they have handed him over to the sheriffs men who are in the village,' answered Kathryn.

'I must thank Edward and go and see the sheriff's men to ensure justice is done.'

'Edmund gave the blacksmith some money,' said Kathryn. 'He handled the whole situation in a very mature manner; I forgot he was my younger brother.'

'I will make sure I thank him too when I see him,' said Thomas. 'I can see you are in capable hands so I will ride on to the village,' and he remounted his horse and rode off. The ladies continued their journey to the Hall and Mary and Margaret helped Kathryn up the stairs to lie down and rest.

Back at the fair Edmund and Matilda were enjoying themselves watching a pair of jugglers with Francis and Richard.

'I see that a cockfight is about to begin, can we go and see it father?' asked Edmund.

'It is not suitable for your sister,' said his father, 'and I do not want you to go alone.'

'Why can't I see it?' asked Matilda.

'You are a young lady and I do not think you mother would be pleased if I let you mix with the sort of people that go to a cockfight'.

'You would not like it Matilda, I know I don't. I could look after Matilda for you if you wish to go,' said Francis to Richard.

'If it is not too much trouble Brother Francis,' replied Richard.

Matilda was happy with the arrangement and said to Francis.

'I would like to buy Kathryn the comb she chose before her purse was stolen.'

'Then that is what we shall do,' said Francis and he took Matilda's hand and they went to find the peddler.

'I suppose in that case I have no excuse not to go with you to see the cocks fighting,' said Richard to his son and they set off towards the cockfight.

There was a large crowd, mainly men surrounding the cockpit and Richard and Edmund found a space with difficulty.

'Keep a tight hold on your money Edmund, there will be pickpockets in this crowd,' said Richard. Someone tapped him on the shoulder and he turned round, it was Thomas.

'I didn't expect to see you here,' shouted Thomas. 'Have you placed a bet?'

'No we are only here to look, Edmund wanted to see a fight as he has never seen one before,' said Richard.

'Edmund, I understand I must thank you for

apprehending the thief who stole my wife's purse. Let me place a bet for you in gratitude. Which one do you fancy?'

'The scrawny one,' said Edmund decisively, and Thomas went to place the bet.

The cockerels' owners placed them in the pit. The larger one immediately attacked the small one and drew blood but it quickly recovered and retaliated. It was difficult to see which was winning and the noise of the spectators was deafening as they shouted encouragement for their cockerel. The fight lasted for about five minutes and it was noticeable that the larger one was tiring. Edmund was shouting himself hoarse and finally the scrawny one went in for kill and won the fight.

'You must go and collect your winnings Edmund,' said Richard and he did so, returning very pleased with himself.

'I shall buy us all a drink,' he declared and they all went over to the stall that sold ale and he purchased three jugs of ale. Matilda and Francis found them there and Matilda showed her father her purchases.

'Look father, aren't they pretty,' she said. 'Francis offered to pay but I would not let him.'

'They are very pretty dear,' said her father. 'I think it is time we were going home now. Are you coming with us Thomas?'

'No, I want to find the sheriff's men to, check

they have Kathryn's attacker safe and then I will go to the smithy to thank Edward Smithson. Would you like to come with me Edmund?'

'Yes please,' said Edmund, and he went off with Thomas.

'Matilda and I will walk back to the Hall,' said Richard. 'Thank you for all you have done today, Brother Francis, it has been a pleasure to meet you.' He shook Francis's hand and he and Matilda left to return to the Hall.

The rest of the Leys' visit to Chadsbury Hall was very quiet. Kathryn spent most of the time resting in the solar talking to her parents and when they left two days later the swelling of her ankle had abated and she was able to walk on it.

Their goodbyes were tearful but Thomas promised to bring Kathryn to Kilborough on a visit in the near future.

Chapter 23

Jake returned to Chadsbury Green early on Thursday morning. He had driven Anne home, she had invited him in for coffee and he had ended up staying all night. They had made love and slept together in Anne's bed and it was this that he was thinking of as he drove into the village. His thoughts elsewhere he did not at first see the police car stopped in the road but he managed to slam his brakes on just in time and narrowly avoided driving into the back of it. Inside the car were Sergeant Bridges and a young police officer and they both got out and came over to Jake.

'Oh, Hello Jake,' said Sergeant Bridges. 'You're out early this morning. That was a near miss.'

'Good Morning, Sergeant Bridges. I'm sorry, I was miles away. I didn't expect to see anyone on the road so early,' replied Jake.

'Well there's no harm done,' said the sergeant. 'We are just going into the village to help clear up, our investigation is over now.'

'You mean you have found who killed Mr Shah?' asked Jake.

'Yes, someone has been charged so you can all rest easy in your beds.'

'Can you tell me who?' asked Jake.

'I don't see why not as it will be on the early morning news,' replied the sergeant and proceeded to tell him.

Jake drove into the yard at the side of the house and raced into the kitchen. The family was all sitting down to breakfast.

'What time do you call this then?' asked George Allen, winking at his wife.

'Never mind that dad, have you had the news on yet? Mrs Shah murdered her husband!' said Jake. They were speechless and then Mrs Allen said,

'I can't believe it, that nice young woman.'

'Well it's true,' said Jake. 'I just bumped into Sergeant Bridges, well almost, and he said that they had charged her with the murder and her brothers helped her dispose of the body.'

'They didn't do a very good job of it, it wasn't very well hidden,' said George. 'Put the radio on Doreen and we will see if it is on the local news.' While they were waiting for the news bulletin Jake told them what Sergeant Bridges had said.

'Mrs Shah confessed to them; she said that she was very unhappy and that night they had a row and she stabbed him with a kitchen knife,' said Jake. 'She then called her brothers and they drove over from Leicester, removed the body from the house, dumped it and returned to their homes.'

'It would have made more sense to take the body a bit further afield wouldn't you think?' said George.

'What will happen to her?' asked Doreen.

'I suppose there will be a trial and she will go to gaol,' said George. 'Be quiet, I think the news is about to start,' and they all listened to the radio that reported that Mrs Shah and her two brothers were to be charged with the murder.

George and Jake left for work, dropping Jenny off at the stables on their way. As they were leaving the stables they saw Rissa arriving and slowed down.

'Have you heard the news?' asked Rissa. 'Isn't it awful, Jackie just didn't seem the type.'

'Well, you never know what happens between husband and wife when they are at home,' said George. 'I doubt living with Dezi Shah was great fun.'

'But even so, to kill him,' said Rissa. 'I hope I never feel that way about Simon.'

'I'm sure you won't,' reassured George.

'I thought I had better let you know that I will be round to check on the carpet fitters at lunchtime George, if you need me you know where I am,' and Rissa drove into the stable yard.

George and Jake arrived at Brook House, let the carpet fitters in and then continued working on the patio. Just as they were about to break for lunch Anne James arrived on her motor bike.

'Hello Mr Allen,' she said. 'I did enjoy myself yesterday evening.'

'I'm sure you did my dear, and please call me

George,' he said. She blushed.

'Your wife is an excellent cook. Hello Jake.'

'Don't mind dad,' he said. 'What are you here for anyway, not that it isn't nice to see you?'

'I called Rissa and she said she was coming over here. The bone expert has been and I wanted to tell her what he said. She suggested we had lunch at the pub.' As she finished speaking Rissa arrived.

'Hello everyone, I will just check on the fitters Anne, and then we can go to lunch. Why don't you go down to the Angel with Jake and I will join you.' she said.

'I may have a quick one too,' said George. 'We have sandwiches today but I am sure Dawn will turn a blind eye if we eat them at the pub. That is if you don't mind your old dad coming with you?'

'Of course we don't,' said Anne, and they all got in the truck and drove down to the pub.

Rissa went inside to see the how the carpet fitting was progressing. The fitters said that they had just finished for the day. The only carpet that was left to do was the hall and stairs and they would be back the next morning to do that. Rissa walked around the house and was pleased with what she saw; she locked up and went to join the Allen's at the Angel.

Rissa arrived at the pub to find George, Jake and Anne talking to John Mallory at the bar.

'Hello Rissa, we were just saying how sorry we

are to hear about Jackie Shah,' said John.

'I know, isn't it awful, she must have had good reason,' Rissa replied.

'From what I hear her brothers are shady characters; it must run in the family,' said John.

'At least it means that the police are leaving the village and things can get back to normal,' said George. 'I can't say I have enjoyed having the village full of cars and people.'

'From a purely selfish point of view it has been good for business,' John said, 'but poor Dawn has been run off her feet preparing meals and I don't think we have seen the last of the police around here.'

'What do you mean?' asked Anne.

'There is still the question of the missing vicar' replied John. 'I had Susan Harvey in here last night and she is very worried about her brother; she still hasn't heard from him, not that I blame him he isn't very likeable. I expect he has just gone away to escape her whining. He once told me she was trying to persuade him to let her live with him and he wasn't keen.'

'But it has been a long time without a word and he took his duties in the parish very seriously,' said Rissa.

'That's true,' said John. 'As I was saying, Susan was in here and she said that the police were beginning to take her concerns seriously and that they had started a nation-wide search, checking airports and channel ports to see if he had left the country. She said that if they still haven't found him by the beginning of next week they will start to scour the local countryside. That will mean more police in the village again.'

'Let's hope they find him before they have to resort to that,' said George. 'Anyway John, as it is not too busy do you mind if Jake and I eat our sandwiches with our pint?'

'Just this once,' replied John.

'I will have a vegetarian lasagne please John, what about you Anne?' said Rissa.

'The same please,' she replied, and they all moved away from the bar and sat in the corner of the pub.

'You have some news for me about the skeleton?' asked Rissa.

'Yes,' answered Anne. 'Professor Drake, the bone expert came to see me this morning and looked at the skeleton. He agreed with me that from the artefacts found with the body that it was most likely from the 15th century but he has taken the bones away to be analysed. He also said that it was definitely male, probably in his twenties. It was fascinating what he could deduce just from looking at the bones, he said that from the general appearance of the bones that he was not used to manual

214

labour but there was evidence of wear and tear on the knees. That would support my theory that he could be a priest or a monk as they would kneel down a lot to pray.'

'But that's amazing,' exclaimed Rissa. 'I never imagined that you could glean so much information just from looking at bones.'

'But that's not all,' continued Anne. 'The most exciting piece of information he gave me was that he had not died from natural causes! There was evidence of a blow to the head and one of the ribs showed a mark which could have been a cut from a knife, which would imply he was stabbed.'

'So you are saying that he was murdered,' said Rissa. 'The poor man. I would love to know who he was and why he died.'

'We may be able to find out his identity from old records, or he could have just been someone passing through,' said Anne. 'Professor Drake may find out some more and he said that he will return the pilgrim and write me out a full report.'

'I shall ask Granny if she knows of any old documents relating to the church; I was going to call in on her before going back to work anyway;' said Rissa. 'That was good timing, I can see our food is ready,' and she went to collect it from the bar. While they were eating they all continued to talk about the skeleton and Dezi Shah's murder and as they were finishing George said,

'Well, we had better be back to work; do you want a lift back to your bike, Anne?'

'We will walk back Dad,' Jake answered for her. 'We won't be long'.

'You had better not be, I want to finish that patio this week,' said George, and he said goodbye and left to return to work.

'We had better go as well Rissa,' said Jake. 'I don't want to be in trouble with the boss.'

She laughed.

'Who, your dad or me? I will see you soon Jake, and I will see you on Tuesday Anne if not before, you know where we are meeting?'

'Yes I do,' said Anne. 'I am looking forward to it,' and she left the pub with Jake, his arm around her.

Chapter 24

Rissa finished her drink and walked down to her grandmothers. Mary Montagu opened her front door and smiled when she saw her granddaughter on the doorstep.

'Come in Rissa, this is a nice surprise. Doreen Allen is here and we were just having coffee, grab a cup and come and join us in the sun porch.' Rissa followed her grandmother into the house and went into the kitchen for a cup and then went through to the sunny porch where Doreen Allen and Mary were sitting.

'Hello Doreen,' she said. 'I have just had lunch with your husband and son in the Angel'.

'Have you now,' said Doreen. 'I thought they were supposed to be working.'

'Well, Anne came over to tell me about the skeleton and I suggested they joined us. They have gone back to work now.'

'Jake spent the night with Anne again last night. I was just telling your grandmother about her visit last night and what a nice girl she is. Jake seems to like her,' said Doreen.

'Yes, I like her too and they seem to be happy together,' said Rissa.

'There will be the sound of wedding bells in your house next,' said Mary jokingly.

'Oh I think it is a bit soon for that Mary, mind

you the twins were hinting last night. Anne was quite a hit with them,' said Doreen smiling. 'But Rissa, I am sure you didn't come to see your grandmother to talk about Jake and Anne.'

'No dear you must tell us about your skeleton,' said Mary. Rissa proceeded to repeat everything that Anne had told her and when she had finished she said

'I thought Granny that you might know where to look for information on the church. I would like to try and find out who the pilgrim was. I also came to see if you were alright about Jackie Shah.'

'There is a board in the church listing the dates and names of the vicars of the Parish which may be of help, we could walk up there after coffee and have a look if you would like. As to poor Jackie I was quite shocked and I must admit I was wondering what would happen to their house. I liked Jackie but I can't say I would be too pleased if some of her relatives took residence next door.'

'I'm sure that won't happen,' said Rissa reassuringly. 'I would imagine it will stay empty until things are sorted out.'

'You are probably right, not that I would like it to be empty for too long; I always found it reassuring to know that someone was next door,' Mary said.

'You know we are not too far away if you need help,' said Doreen to the older woman.

'Thank you Doreen, you are so kind,' said Mary. 'But I haven't told you Rissa the purpose of Doreen's visit. Anne has invited us to the museum on Saturday. Doreen and I are going to compare our family trees and take them with us to show Anne and then we are going to look around the museum. The twins are also going to come to see the skeleton and afterwards we are taking them to lunch in the burger house so it will be quite an adventure for me.'

'I am sure you will enjoy your visit, but Anne has just told me that Professor Drake has taken the skeleton away to be analysed,' said Rissa.

'Oh dear, the twins will be disappointed. Still, I am sure there will be plenty of other things to see,' said Doreen. 'I must be going, but I will see you tomorrow morning Mary when we do the church flowers. You can come round to mine for coffee afterwards and we can compare our family trees. Good bye Rissa'.

'Goodbye Doreen,' said Mary, and Rissa rose with Doreen and saw her to the front door. When she returned Mary said,

'If you can carry the coffee cups through into the kitchen Rissa, I shall fetch my coat and walk up to the church with you.' Rissa did as she was bid and they locked up the house and walked up the lane to the church.

Mary had a key to the church but when they got

there it was open and they found William Arden there.

'Hello William, we didn't expect to see you here,' said Mary.

'No, well I have been asked to step into the breech until Richard is found. I came up to check on a few things before I prepare Sunday's sermon,' he replied.

'The police are checking the ports and airports to see if there is any trace of him,' said Rissa. 'If he isn't found soon you will be officiating at my wedding.'

'I will be only too pleased to be of service,' answered William.

'You might be able to help us,' said Mary. 'Rissa is still trying to identify her skeleton and we believe it to be the bones of a priest or a monk. I suggested that we came here to look at the board listing the vicars of Chadsbury Green and also see if there were any other documents that could be useful.'

'We are interested in the 15th century,' said Rissa.

'Let me see,' said William thoughtfully. 'The first place is to look at the names on the board. Shall we have a look?' They went over to look at the board and on it were listed all the incumbents of the parish dating back to 1350.

'I suggest you make a note of the names of in the 15th century,' William said.

Rissa took a notebook out of her bag and noted the relevant names and dates:

Joshua Pollard	1415-1420
William Chapman	1420-1432
Henry Wodeward	1432-1458
John Lovell	1458-1471
Richard Palmer	1471-1479

'But I'm still none the wiser as to the identity of the pilgrim,' sighed Rissa.

'You may be,' said William. 'James Trent, a vicar here in the 18th century, was very interested in the history of the church and the lives of those that preceded him and he wrote a book about the church. I seem to remember it was kept in the vestry. Shall we go and look?' They followed William into the vestry and he went over to the bookshelf and looked at the books there.

'I've found it,' he cried. 'I knew it was here, perhaps you should take it away with you and read it Rissa, you may find what you are looking for.'

'That's a good idea,' said Rissa. 'I shall take great care of it.'

'You have been a great help,' said Mary. 'When you have finished here perhaps you would like to come and visit me for a cup of tea?'

'It would be a pleasure,' replied William.

'I had better get back to work, thanks for the book,' said Rissa, and she picked up the book, left the church and returned to her car.

Rissa spent the rest of the afternoon at the stables and in the evening she spoke to Simon on the phone and invited him to spend the weekend at the Hall so that they could make a start on cleaning their new house and moving furniture. When she had finished her telephone call she took the book she had borrowed from the church to her room to read. She looked for the names of the priests she had made a note of in the book and found that four of them were mentioned. There was only a brief note about Joshua Pollard he had only been there for 5 years at the end of his life and he had died at the age of sixty. William Chapman who had been the incumbent for 12 years had been in his middle age when he was at Chadsbury Green and he had then moved onto a neighbouring parish. There was no mention of Richard Palmer but a whole chapter devoted to Henry Wodewarde and John Lovell. She settled down to read this with interest and became quite excited when she read about Henry Wodewarde. He had been at Chadsbury Green for twenty-six years and during that time a school had been started in the village. It was also recorded that his young nephew, a monk, had spent a year in the village before returning to his monastery in the north of England. Rissa hurriedly looked through the rest of the book but she could find neither further mention of the monk, his name nor which monastery he belonged to but she wondered if the skeleton they had found could possibly be that of Henry Wodewarde's nephew!

Chapter 25

As William Aleyn strolled through the village he was feeling very pleased with himself. He had just agreed with Joshua Makepeace that Richard would marry Molly in the spring, it had been a successful harvest, and he had been able to put provisions down for the winter and pay his dues to the lord of the manor. 'Now all I need to do now is secure the position of bailiff and life will be perfect,' he thought. Roger Tyler had decided he wanted to retire before the winter and he promised to recommend William as his successor.

As William walked past the church he saw Francis emerge and make his way up the lane to the Hall. 'It must be his day for visiting Lady Kathryn,' he mused.

William had watched Francis and Kathryn a number of times since the episode by the river but it had always been from some way off. Today, he decided, he would follow Francis and see what he got up to. Keeping at a safe distance he trailed Francis to the Hall, and then crouched in some bushes near the entrance and waited. He didn't have to wait long. Francis and Kathryn came out of the house and walked down the drive past the bushes in which William was hiding. He followed them stealthily. They were talking and laughing and never noticed William as he stalked them darting from hiding place to hiding place. They strolled down to the river and walked beside it until they reached a point where the rushes were high and when they sat down they were hidden from view. William crossed to the other side of the river and made his way on the opposite bank to where they were sitting and chose a suitable vantage point from which he could observe them without being seen.

Francis and Kathryn had continued with their lessons throughout the summer. Every week they spent one of these lessons out of doors and everyone had become accustomed to seeing the pair out together. One of their favourite spots was the riverbank - it was rare to see anyone else there during the day as they were all busy in the fields. During these walks Francis did spend some of the time teaching Kathryn but most of the time was spent exploring each other's bodies and getting to know each others as young lovers do.

'I have some news for you,' said Kathryn her eyes sparkling. 'I am with child; I am going to have your baby.'

Francis was stunned and could not speak. His mind was a whirl of thoughts and feelings from elation to horror. Finally he managed to say,

'How do you know it is mine, it could be your husbands?'

Kathryn smiled knowingly.

'A woman knows these things; besides, I never

fell with child in those many months of my marriage before I met you. I think we made the child the first time we lay together in the woods.'

Francis did not know what else to say.

'Did you not guess? My breasts are larger and my stomach is beginning to swell.'

'I have no experience of these things,' said Francis. 'Are you taking care of yourself, I do know that you must not over exert yourself in the first few months. We should not have walked so far today.'

'Everything is fine Francis. Would you like to see my breasts and feel how they have changed,' and she undid her dress, took his hand and placed it over her breast. 'Can you not feel the change in them?'

Francis slowly moved his hand across her breasts, caressing them and feeling their fullness. He then moved his hand further down and felt the soft swelling of her stomach. He bent down and kissed it.

'You look beautiful,' he said and he could feel himself stirring with desire.

'You too are beautiful Francis,' said Kathryn, and she settled down in the rushes making herself more comfortable, and pulled him down with her.

William on the other side of the river could not believe his eyes. He had caught a glimpse of Kathryn's breasts and he saw the monk caress and kiss them and then his view was obscured as they lay hidden in the rushes but he could hear the noise of their lovemaking. He felt himself become aroused and wished that he could take the place of the monk. He had seen enough and crept away thinking as he did so how best to use this knowledge. 'It is a pity I could not hear what they said,' he thought.

After they had made love Kathryn and Francis lay on their backs amongst the reeds enjoying the sunshine.

'What will we do?' asked Francis.

'I don't know,' said Kathryn.

'I could ask you to run away with me but where would we go and what would we live on, a disgraced monk and a lady?'

'We could go to France; no one would ever find us there. You could teach and I could care for you and our child.'

'I couldn't ask that of you, it would mean that you would never see your family again, we would be poor and you are not accustomed to that.'

'I would live anywhere if I was with you.'

'But what of the child, do you not want what is best for it? If you stay at Chadsbury Hall you and the child will never want for anything. These other thoughts can only be in our dreams,' said Francis sadly.

'If I stay what would you do?'

'I would return to my monastery as was the original intention and continue to serve God as best I could.'

'But that would mean I would never see you again and I could not bear that,' and she burst into tears.

'Don't cry, Kathryn,' he said, taking her in his arms once again. 'We will work something out and talk again some other day,' but even as he spoke he knew that their love was doomed and they could never be together. 'Have you told anyone of the child?'

'No, I wanted you to be the first. I will have to tell them soon; I think Lady Viola already suspects but she has not said anything,' said Kathryn, as she remembered that morning when she had left the room quickly to be violently sick. When she had returned Viola had asked if she was sickening for something but Kathryn had just said she thought it must have been something she ate.

'We must go back soon,' said Francis.

'Not just yet,' said Kathryn as she kissed him and her hand moved down between his legs. 'Make love to me one more time,' and Francis placed himself on top of her and carefully entered her. They moved together in harmony and Kathryn clung to him until they climaxed almost together. He rolled away from her and they quickly dressed, and he helped her to stand, brushing her clothes and removing seeds from her hair. They held each other in one last passionate embrace and as they walked home they talked together in French.

On his way back to the village William Aleyn pondered on what he had seen and listed the possibilities with which he could use the information to his advantage. He dismissed the idea of speaking to the monk as he could not see any benefit from doing so. He considered confronting Kathryn but was unsure of her influence with her husband. That left two possible candidates, to whom he could impart the information; these were her husband Sir Thomas de Montagu or Lady Viola de Montagu. He decided on the latter. Sir Thomas may be the one to make decision about the bailiff's job but he may not believe in his wife's infidelity and his anger could turn on William. Lady Viola on the other hand was a shrewd woman with a lot of influence with her son, he felt sure she would listen to him and act on his information as he would wish. He decided that he would not speak to her just yet but would bide his time and wait for a suitable moment.

Chapter 26

Doreen and Mary had spent Friday morning arranging the church flowers and comparing notes on their family trees. They had found a lot of connections between the two families and they were both quite excited about showing Anne the results they had achieved.

Doreen and the twins picked Mary up early on Saturday morning and they drove into Kilborough. Sophie seemed to have recovered from her ordeal and Doreen said that she had slept through last night without a nightmare. Both girls seemed to accept that Jackie Shah had killed her husband quite easily. They chattered quite happily in the back of the car and Mary was content to just sit quietly and listen to them. When they arrived at the museum Anne was in the foyer to meet them. Sophie and Nicola greeted her with enthusiasm and Doreen introduced Mary.

'It's a pleasure to meet you my dear,' said Mary. 'My granddaughter has talked a lot about you.'

'Jake never stops talking about you,' said Sophie.

Anne shook Mary's hand and turned to the twins.

'I hope you won't be disappointed but the skeleton isn't here; it has gone away for analysis but the museum has some other skeletons and also some mummies which should interest you. John has offered to show you round,' and as she said this a young man came down the stairs. 'John, this is Sophie and Nicola who I was telling you about.'

John who was on a year's secondment to the museum from university smiled at the twins.

'Hello ladies,' he said. 'I am under orders to show you the more gruesome artefacts that the museum has on display, is that OK?'

'That sounds great,' chorused the twins and they followed John into the museum.

'If you would like to come in here you can show me your family trees and then if you would like I can show you some of the things in the museum that may be of more interest to you,' said Anne. She showed Mary and Doreen into a small conference room off the main foyer.

They sat down at a large table and each of the ladies laid out their family trees.

'When we got together yesterday and compared them we found that both families have been in the village for a long time,' said Doreen. 'But as yet we haven't found any evidence that they are related. The Allen family were always labourers or artisans and the Montagues the gentry.'

'I have managed to trace the Montague family through the centuries and with the help of the documents you gave Rissa I have made the connection between the de Montagu and the Montague family,' said Mary. 'What I find really fascinating is the use of the same Christian names through the ages. For the men Thomas, Harold and Francis seem to be popular and for the woman Margaret and Kathryn.'

'I too have made the connection between Allen and Aleyn. It appears that the family started as serfs, and there were then three generations of bailiffs to the de Montagu family. The following generations were craftsmen connected with the building trade,' Doreen added.

'Chadsbury Hall and its estates have been handed down through the family for generations and it has quite easy to trace the immediate line,' continued Mary. 'But I am very interested at finding out more about other branches of the family. In my searches I have come across Montagues who have been in the army and one younger son in the 18th century was a sea captain.'

Anne studied the work that the two ladies had done and then she said.

'I am very impressed, this must have taken a lot of hard work and if you continue to expand them it could get very complicated.'

'I realise that but I enjoy it,' said Mary. 'I am learning new things about the family every day.'

'I have enjoyed doing it too,' said Doreen.

'If you would like I will show you round the museum,' said Anne. 'I thought you would be interested in the old kitchen tools we have on display here and also some of our archive material relating to Chadsbury Green and the surrounding area. Unless you have anything else you would particularly like to see?'

'No what you described sounds just right,' said Doreen, and the two ladies followed Anne out of the door for a guided tour of the museum.

When they had finished they returned to the conference room. There were sounds of laughter coming from inside the room and Anne opened the door and found Nicola and Sophie with John waiting for them.

'Hi mum,' said Nicola. 'We have had a great time; we even saw a pickled monkey brain.'

'Yes, it's been great, I liked the stuffed animals best,' added Sophie.

'I hope they haven't been too much of a trial for you,' said Doreen to John.

'No, I enjoyed showing them round,' he said.

'He has just been telling us a funny story about when he fell in a trench full of mud on a dig,' said Nicola.

'Well, we must thank you both for your hospitality and leave you to get on with your work,' said Doreen. 'Unless you want to come with us for lunch at the burger house?'

'You must come, Anne,' said Sophie.

'And you John,' added Nicola.

Anne looked at John who nodded and she said,

'We would be delighted, I have finished for today and John is due a lunch break, I will just go and collect my coat and bag.'

When Rissa returned they all left the museum and walked through the town to the burger bar. As it was a Saturday the restaurant was very busy, but John spotted a free table and he went over to it and sat down as the others followed.

'This is my treat,' said Doreen. 'What would you all like?'

'I haven't a clue,' said Mary. The twins proceeded to tell Mary what was on offer and she said that she would try a 'Superburger'. Mary stayed at the table and the rest went across to the counter and placed their orders. They didn't take long and came back with the burgers, chips and drinks.

'This is really quite good,' declared Mary. 'But I would have liked a knife and fork.' Everyone laughed and Doreen said,

'But it does save on the washing up.'

When she had finished eating Mary said to Anne.

'Have you spoken to Rissa recently?'

'No, not since I saw her on Thursday.'

'She came to see me after your lunch and we went to the church. An old friend of mine was there, William Arden; he used to be the vicar of Chadsbury Green. He found Rissa a book on the history of the church and its priests and she took it away to read. Yesterday I was speaking to her and she said that she might have found a possible candidate for the pilgrim. One of the priests in the 15th century was visited by his nephew, a monk. However this young monk returned to his monastery in the north of England.'

'So how can he be the one we found?' asked Anne.

'Well Rissa's theory is that he may never have returned to his monastery but as she doesn't know his name or his monastery we may never know, but she is convinced that he is the one.'

'An interesting theory,' said Anne. 'But as you say, difficult to prove.'

As everyone had now finished their meal they all said their goodbyes and went their separate ways.

Chapter 27

It had been a week since Kathryn had told Francis about their baby and every morning since then she had been sick. This morning she was walking in the kitchen garden when a wave of nausea overcame her, and she rushed over to a corner of the garden and was sick. She supported herself on the apple tree recovering from her efforts when she felt a hand on her arm; she turned round quickly to find that it was Viola.

'What's troubling you Kathryn?' asked Viola with concern. 'Are you with child?'

Kathryn realised that she could keep her secret from Viola no longer and said,

'Yes.' Her mother in law gently led her over to a bench in the sun and they sat down.

'But that is wonderful news Kathryn, have you told my son yet?' Viola asked.

'No, I wanted to be sure before I told him,' said Kathryn.

'Well, I have suspected it for a few days now but I did not say anything. I was hoping you would confide in me. An heir for the de Montagu family - I had almost given up hope!'

Kathryn burst into tears and her mother-in law took her in her arms.

'But you should not be crying this is a time to rejoice,' said Viola.

'I know,' whispered Kathryn. 'But I am so afraid.'

'You are young and healthy there is nothing for you to be afraid of. Come, you must dry your tears and go and tell your husband the good news.'

Kathryn looked at the older woman and longed to confide in her, but knew that she could not. Viola would not be so sympathetic if she knew of Kathryn's treachery.

'I suppose you think I am silly,' said Kathryn. 'I seem so tired and I have been sick every morning for the last two weeks.'

'No, I don't think you are silly, all women suffer like this. You will find that in a few weeks you will feel much better. Perhaps you should not do so much work in the house and stop your lessons with Brother Francis if they tire you.'

Kathryn looked at Viola, the alarm showing clearly on her face and she stood up quickly, saying,

'No, I am feeling much better now and I would not want to stop my lessons with Brother Francis. I enjoy them and he is a good friend.'

'Well, we shall see, but you have so much to look forward to and to plan. Dry your tears and go and tell Thomas the good news.' Kathryn went in search of her husband, leaving Viola sitting on the bench.

Viola watched her daughter-in-law leave the garden and pondered over the news that Kathryn had reluctantly told her. She had given up all hope that Thomas would ever have an heir and she was pleased to hear that Kathryn was with child. At the same time she was concerned about Kathryn and her reaction to the suggestion that she curtailed her lessons with Brother Francis. Viola thought her son had been too lax with his young wife, allowing the friendship to develop between her and Brother Francis. She had broached the subject with her son but he had said he was pleased with the monk and Kathryn. He said that he found his wife to be a more agreeable companion since she had started her lessons with Brother Francis and he was quite happy for them to continue. Viola was still suspicious, and her conversation with Kathryn that morning led her to wonder if the child was perhaps not her son's. She tried to reassure herself that this could not be the case, but she also vowed to keep a closer eye on Kathryn when Brother Francis visited.

Kathryn found her husband in the stables about to leave for a days hunting.

'Could I speak with you?' she asked.

'If it's quick,' said Thomas impatiently. 'I was just about to leave.'

'I was hoping to speak to you in private,' said Kathryn. 'It is important.'

'Oh very well,' snapped Thomas, and he dismounted from his horse. He took hold of his wife's arm and walked her to the edge of the stable block out of earshot of the servants.

'Well, what do you have to say that is so important?' he seemed angry and he frightened Kathryn but she cleared her throat and said timidly.

'I have some news that should please you, husband. I am with child.'

The change in his face was almost instantaneous, his look transformed from one of anger to one of pure joy.

'Did you say you are with child Kathryn?'

'Yes, I am going to give you an heir,' she said. Thomas picked her up and swung her round in the air and kissed her on the lips before gently putting her down again.

'You have made me so happy,' he said. 'We must tell everyone.'

'I am glad you are pleased,' said Kathryn. 'But I would rather we did not tell everyone just yet. Your mother knows; she guessed but let's keep it a secret from everyone else for a few weeks yet until I know the baby is safe.'

'If that is what you want,' said Thomas. 'I will now go out to hunt a happy man and I shall see you this evening,' and he returned to his horse with a big smile on his face. He remounted and rode off, waving to Kathryn as he did so.

Kathryn watched him go and gave a sigh of relief. The news of her baby would not be public knowledge for some time yet and she could pretend that nothing had changed. She knew that she had some difficult decisions to make, but she could at least postpone them for a few more days yet. This afternoon Francis was coming and it was the day of their weekly walk.

When Francis arrived at Chadsbury Hall for his lesson with Kathryn, Viola intercepted him at the door.

'Good day, Brother Francis,' she said. 'I see you here again for another lesson with Lady Kathryn. I trust that she is doing well at her lessons.'

'Good day, Lady Viola, Lady Kathryn is a very talented young lady I am very pleased with her.'

'A married lady,' said Viola, her meaning clear. At that moment Kathryn arrived and saved Francis from replying.

'Hello, Brother Francis,' she said. 'It is another lovely day I shall enjoy a walk in the fresh air.'

'You are going for a walk?' asked Viola.

'Yes,' said Kathryn. 'We do every week; I have my lesson as we walk.'

'Don't tire yourself,' said Viola. 'You know you must take care.'

'I shall look after her,' said Francis, and they made their excuses and went out into the sunshine and walked down the drive of the Hall.

Viola watched them go, convinced now that her suspicions were correct.

'Lady Viola knows about the child,' said Kathryn to Francis. 'She saw me being sick this morning and asked me. I had to tell her and then I told my husband. He was overjoyed. I have asked him not to tell anyone else just yet.'

'You were sick?' queried Francis.

'Oh it is nothing to worry about, it happens at first in the mornings,' said Kathryn. 'Where shall we go for our walk?'

'I thought we would go to the river again,' he said smiling at her, and then he frowned as he saw William Aleyn working towards them.

'Good afternoon Lady Kathryn and Brother Francis, nice day for a walk,' said Aleyn, and he winked at Francis. They both nodded at him and continued walking.

'I don't like him,' said Kathryn when he was out of earshot.

'No, neither do I,' concurred Francis, wondering why Aleyn had winked at him, and they increased their pace so that they could reach the privacy of the river bank quicker.

Chapter 28

William Aleyn reached Chadsbury Hall and asked if he could speak with Lady Viola. He had finally plucked up courage to broach the subject of the bailiff's job with her. A servant invited him into the hall and said that Lady Viola would speak to him there.

'Good day, William, what do you wish to speak to me about?' Asked Lady Viola when she came into the hall.

'Good day my lady, thank you for taking the time to speak to me,' said William as he bowed to her. 'I have two matters I wish to discuss with you but you may want to hear the second one somewhere more private.'

Viola looked at William Aleyn carefully. She had never particularly liked the man, he was oily and sly, but she accepted that he was a hard worker. She wondered what he wanted to say to her.

'Well I haven't got all day but I can spare you a few minutes and if you insist that it is private then we can speak in the solar,' she said, and led him into the room. 'Please tell me what you want to say,' she said when they had entered the room and she had closed the door.

'I have some information for you about a member of your family, which could be embarrassing in the wrong hands,' he said.

'What on earth are you talking about?' she demanded.

'Before I tell you I have another matter I wish to discuss,' he whined. 'Roger Tyler hopes to retire this winter and I would like to take his place. I was hoping that you would recommend me to Lord de Montagu.'

'How dare you presume I will do any such thing!' she exclaimed angrily.

Aleyn went on. 'I have been watching Lady Kathryn and Brother Francis these past few weeks.'

The blood drained from Viola's face and she said,

'Please explain yourself; you have no right to be spying on a member of this family.'

'I have seen them going for walks by the river hand in hand and last week I saw them...' he didn't get a chance to say anymore as Viola raised her hand to stop him speaking.

'I do not wish to hear any more of your lies,' she shouted.

'Oh but I think you do, my lady,' said William. His confidence was growing as he could tell that he was scaring the old lady. 'If I become the next bailiff I promise not to tell anyone else that I saw a monk with his hand up the skirt of your son's wife!'

'Enough William, I have heard enough,' she said more quietly than before. 'Leave me now.'

'I shall be back,' he said, then turned and left.

Viola went and sat down in a chair she was shaking with anger and fear. She knew that William was telling the truth and it confirmed her worst fears. Although she had suffered a shock she was a strong woman and quickly recovered. She calmed down and put her mind to the task of solving the problem. Viola could be ruthless when it came to ensuring the safety of the family and its name. She was sure she would find a solution. Her main concern was the child that Kathryn was carrying. The family needed an heir and she could not allow there to be any hint of scandal surrounding its birth. There was no one she could talk to and her son had to believe that the child was his and it must be born at Chadsbury Hall. She needed to make sure that Kathryn did not decide to run off with the monk but remained with her husband to be the Hall's future mistress. Her next problem was to ensure that Francis Wodewarde left the area never to return. Much as she disliked William Aleyn she knew that he would make a good bailiff and she would be able to keep an eye on him. As she sat there she made a number of decisions, the first of which she resolved to act upon that evening.

The evening meal at Chadsbury Hall was a lively affair; Thomas had spoken to Kathryn on his return and persuaded her to let him tell his sister Margaret the good news. He waited until the servants had left the room and then said,

'Margaret, we have something to tell you - Kathryn is with child!'

'I am delighted for you both,' said Margaret. 'Perhaps Thomas, you will allow me to help bring your son into the world?'

'It won't be until next year,' said Kathryn. 'I hope you will be there to help me.'

'Kathryn has asked for us to keep it from the servants for a few more weeks yet and I have reluctantly agreed,' said Thomas.

'Why is that Kathryn?' asked Viola curtly.

Kathryn was surprised at her mother-in-law's tone but answered her.

'I wanted to make sure that all would be well.'

'You have been looking tired, Kathryn,' answered Viola, and then she turned to her son and added 'I am concerned about her and I think she should rest for awhile. I think it would be best if she stopped her lessons with Brother Francis.'

Kathryn felt her heart lurch and she managed to stifle a cry.

'It would be an excellent time for you Kathryn to visit your family in Kilborough,' Viola continued. 'You will find it more difficult nearer your time and I am sure your mother will ensure you do not tire yourself.'

'I agree with you, mother,' said Thomas. 'I shall make the arrangements and take you next week.'

'For how long?' said Kathryn trying to sound

pleased at the suggestion.

'I would suggest you go for at least month,' answered Viola.

'But I will be neglecting my duties here and also my lessons, Thomas,' Kathryn said to her husband, willing him to change his mind.

'I am sure my mother can manage without you and I will ask Brother Francis to set you some simple tasks while you are away if you wish. Your main responsibility is to our child now and preparing for its birth,' he said.

'I am sure Brother Francis has better things to do,' replied Viola curtly. Kathryn was disconcerted by the way Viola was looking at her and she said no more.

The arrangements for Kathryn to visit her parents in Kilborough were quickly made and before she left she only had time for a brief visit with Francis. He came to the Hall at Thomas's request and Kathryn explained to him that she was going away and asked him to set her some work while she was gone. Viola was present for most of this meeting and it was only when he was leaving that Kathryn was able to whisper to him how much she would miss him. Francis told her that he would be thinking about her and they said goodbye.

Chapter 29

Kathryn enjoyed staying with her parents in Kilborough and although she missed Francis and thought of him everyday she soon slipped easily back into her role of the much loved daughter. Her parents were delighted with the news that Kathryn was expecting a child and Mary her mother promised to be with her at the birth. They took great care of Kathryn and she was not allowed to do anything too strenuous. Most days she spent sitting talking to her mother while they stitched clothes and bedding for the new baby. She also went on short early morning walks by herself or with her brother and sister and she rediscovered her love of the sounds of smells of Kilborough.

One day she left the house with her sister to visit the market and as they were walking round the stalls she heard someone call her name.

'Lady Kathryn and Miss Leys if I am not mistaken! This is a pleasant surprise!' Henry Wodewarde hurried over to meet them.

'The surprise is ours Father, what brings you to town?' asked Kathryn.

'I needed some provisions which I cannot obtain in Chadsbury Green and Francis also needed some materials for his school. We have come for a few days and are staying at the church.

'Brother Francis is here?' exclaimed Matilda.

'Where is he? I would like to see him again.'

'He is here somewhere,' said Henry, looking round. 'Ah there he is,' and he called him over.

Francis came over to meet them and said,

'You look well Lady Kathryn, and Matilda - I am sure you have grown since I last saw you!'

Matilda giggled and took hold of his hand.

'I have lots to tell you, would you and your uncle care to come home with us for some refreshment?'

'That would be very kind of you,' he said.

'You walk ahead with Father Wodewarde,' said Kathryn to her sister. 'I would like to discuss my lessons with Brother Francis.' She saw the petulant scowl that Matilda gave her and she smiled and said, 'I promise that when we reach home he is all yours.'

Matilda reluctantly walked on ahead with Henry Wodewarde, and Kathryn and Francis followed slowly behind.

'How have you been Kathryn?' Francis asked.

'I am well,' she replied. 'My visit here has done me some good but I have thought of you every day.'

'I have missed you too, but I have been kept busy teaching the children and praying,' said Francis. 'I have been thinking very seriously about our future and I have made some decisions which I would like to share with you.'

'I also have been doing some thinking,' said

Kathryn. 'We need to talk. Every morning I go for a walk early. Tomorrow morning could you meet me at sunrise by the bridge over the river?'

'Yes I can do that,' he said and they hurried to catch up with his uncle and Matilda before reaching the house.

Mary Leys welcomed their visitors and when they had sat down she went to the kitchen and returned with some of her home-made cordial.

'Lady Kathryn is looking well,' Henry said to her. 'Sir Thomas has told us about the expected child and everyone in the village is looking forward to a new generation of de Montagus'.

'When are you returning home?' asked Francis.

'We have enjoyed having her here so much that we have persuaded her husband to allow her to stay with us until early October,' her mother answered for her.

They then continued to talk about other matters and Matilda took Francis into the kitchen to see the new kittens. After about an hour Henry and Francis thanked Mary for her hospitality but said that they must go and continue with their chores in Kilborough.

The next morning Kathryn was awake very early and she dressed quietly and stole out of the house before anyone else woke up. She arrived at the bridge to find Francis waiting for her.

'I could not sleep,' he said.

'Neither could I,' she answered. 'Follow me and I will take you on my favourite walk.'

He followed her silently as she climbed down onto the path by the riverbank and walked along it away from the town. The river went round a bend and the town was no longer in view, Kathryn took a path that led away from the river up a small hill, at the top she sat down and Francis sat beside her.

'Just look at the view from here,' she said. They could see the river meandering its way through the countryside below.

'It is beautiful,' he replied. 'But should you have walked this far?'

'I have never felt healthier, the exercise is good for me and we need to be alone,' she said as she moved closer to him. He put his arm around her and kissed her on the lips.

'As you can feel I am much bigger now,' she said softly and took his hand and placed it on her stomach. 'That is our baby growing in there.'

'It feels so strange,' he said and then removed his hand. 'But we need to talk and seeing you like this does not make what I have to say very easy.'

'I know it is not easy,' she said. 'Perhaps I should speak first.'

'No, let me say what I have to,' said Francis. 'I never thought that I would ever feel the way that I do Kathryn, I love you with all my heart, body and soul. When I promised myself to God I never knew what I would be missing and it was only when I met you that I knew the true meaning of bodily love. However our love has been doomed from the start. We talked of running away together and starting a new life together with the child but I could never subject you and our child to that kind of life. I could not take you away from your family and your comfortable home to live in poverty, always on the run - you would grow to hate and resent me. I have decided that for your sake and the sake of the child's I must give you up and allow you to live the life to which you were born. I shall return to my monastery and try and live the life I had before I met you.' The tears shone in his eyes as he finished speaking and he turned away from her and wiped his eyes on the sleeve of his habit. 'I am sorry Kathryn that I am a coward and not brave enough to risk a life with you.'

Kathryn too was near to tears as she said,

'You are not a coward Francis, you are the bravest man I know. I love you and that love will be forever. I too have thought about our future while I have been staying here. I have admitted to myself that I am too scared to come away with you. I don't want to leave my family or my comfortable home and I agree with you that in time I would possibly blame you for the hardships we would have to endure. I have also considered what it would be like for you denied your true vocation. Your vows to God are important to you and to live in sin with me and without God would make you very miserable and in turn you would blame me. I have decided that I must sacrifice you for the sake of our child. I want him to grow up surrounded by love, comfort and security and at Chadsbury Hall I can ensure he will receive it.' At the end of this speech the tears were streaming down her face and Francis put his arms around her once more and they clung together comforting each other.

'At least we have both reached the same conclusion,' said Francis eventually.

'I know, but it is going to be so hard never to see you again.' Kathryn's voice broke with emotion.

'But you will have our child to remember me by, whereas I shall only have my memories,' he said ruefully.

'Will you not come and visit your uncle again?' she asked.

'I don't think that would be wise, do you?'

'I suppose not, but I shall see you before you leave?'

'No, I think it would be best if I left before you return or I may weaken.'

'So this is goodbye? I will never forget you Francis,' she whispered. 'Will you do one last thing for me?'

'And what is that?'

'Make love to me one last time.'

'But will we not harm the baby?'

'No, he will be safe,' she said, and Francis laid her down in the grass and they made love. He was very gentle with her and as he reached his climax he opened his eyes and watched as his tears joined hers.

Chapter 30

As planned, Simon had spent the weekend at Chadsbury Hall with Rissa cleaning their new house, hanging curtains and moving furniture. It was now Tuesday evening and Rissa was getting ready for her hen night. She put the finishing touches to her makeup, collected her evening bag and walked down the stairs to the first landing. She met Sarah at the top of the stairs and they both walked down the remaining staircase together. Rissa's father, brother and sister were waiting in the hall and as they approached them Harry gave a low wolf whistle.

'Wow mum, you and sis look really great,' he said - a great complement from a ten-year old.

'I must say I agree with him, I am not sure I should allow you two ladies out alone this evening,' said Tom jokingly. Rissa was dressed in her favourite black velvet jeans; with which she wore a silver camisole with a matching cardigan and high black strappy sandals. She had her hair tied up in a high ponytail. Her mother-in-law Sarah was wearing a bronze trouser suit, the trousers were narrow legged and the jacket had a Nehru style collar and came to below the knee.

'Thanks for the complements,' said Rissa. 'I thought I had better wear trousers - I suspect Fay has something awful planned for me!'

'I wish I was coming,' said Lucy. 'I'm a hen.'

They all laughed and her mother bent down to kiss her and whispered,

'You're still my little chicken.' Sarah then tried to kiss her son goodbye but he managed to avoid it, saying goodbye and fleeing back upstairs to watch television.

'Are you ready ladies? Your carriage awaits,' said Tom and he took his wife's arm and they all walked out to the car. On the way they stopped at the Allen's house to pick up Jenny and Jane.

'Hello everyone,' said Jane as she and her sister got in the car. 'It seems ages since I last saw you Rissa, my shift work plays havoc with my social life.'

'I hope you are not working on Saturday,' said Rissa.

'No I don't go back now until Sunday evening, I shall enjoy the rest. Jenny tells me Jake's new girl-friend will be there tonight - I must admit to being curious, I have never seen my younger brother so smitten about anything other than his bike.'

'He has told us to make sure she behaves tonight,' added Jenny. 'But I for one shall turn a blind eye.'

'I thought this was just a meal at a restaurant,' interrupted Tom from the front of the car.

'There is a dance floor dad, but we will probably have to dance with each other,' said Rissa.

'Don't worry Tom, I shall make sure they all

behave,' said his wife.

'It's not them I'm worried about,' he said, but he smiled at his wife as he said it and she patted his arm, kissed him on the cheek and told him he was the only one for her.

'Well if you are all set then I'll take you into Kilborough. It's the Hare and Hounds isn't it?' he asked.

'Yes,' said Sarah. 'We are meeting everyone there and then we will walk to the restaurant. Don't worry about collecting us; we can share a taxi home'. Tom released the handbrake and drove them to Kilborough. When they reached the Hare and Hounds Tom parked the car and they all got out.

'If I'm not intruding,' he said. 'I would like to come in with you and buy you all a drink, its not often I get a chance to be surrounded by a bevy of beautiful women.'

'Of course you can come in with us dad,' said Rissa. They entered the pub and looked around. It was very old and instead of one large bar there were numerous small rooms and alcoves.

'Sarah and I will go to the bar, while you look for the others,' said Tom. They found Fay sitting with two of Rissa's friends, Simone and Cathy in a tiny room that was filled with squashy armchairs. They all greeted each other and Rissa, Jenny and Jane sat down with the others.

'Sarah and my father have gone to the bar, he insisted on joining us for a drink,' said Rissa.

'Oh good,' said Simone. 'I have always thought your dad was really sexy.' Everyone laughed and they were still laughing when Sarah and Tom found them.

'What are you laughing at?' asked Sarah.

'Don't you dare tell her' said Simone blushing.

'Simone was just remarking on the local talent,' said Rissa, which caused Fay and Cathy to have another fit of the giggles.

'I guessed I must be in the right place, I heard a lot of girlish laughter,' said Ruth, another old school friend of Rissa's. As she entered the room she was followed by Anne, and Rissa made the introductions.

'I thought you were buying the drinks, dad,' said Rissa.

'I have,' he replied. 'They said they would bring them over,' and as he finished speaking a barman came in carrying an ice bucket and two bottles of champagne.

'Here you are Sir; I will just go and get the glasses,' the barman said.

'Dad, you shouldn't have,' exclaimed Rissa.

'I wanted my little girl's party to start off well, so I ordered it earlier,' he said. The barman returned with the glasses and Tom popped the cork and poured it.

'I would like to propose a toast to my beautiful wife and daughter and all the other lovely ladies here, I hope you have a very enjoyable evening,' Tom said and they all agreed and drank. When he had finished his drink Tom said,

'I don't want to spoil your fun so I will leave you to it,' and he kissed Sarah and Rissa, but before they would let him leave all the other girls insisted on giving him a kiss as well, at which point he finally escaped from the pub.

They all sat and sipped their champagne and talked, making admiring noises about each others' outfits. Fay was dressed in a long black halter neck dress with a slit up one side and Anne was wearing a short midnight blue dress with very small straps.

'You look very different,' said Rissa.

'I hope you like it,' said Anne 'I bought it today, I needed to buy something for your wedding and I saw this and had to have it as well.'

'Jake will approve,' said Jenny admiringly.

'If we have all finished complimenting each other perhaps we should give Rissa her present,' said Fay, and she produced a large box from under the table. 'This is for you from all of us Rissa,' she said, and handed her the box. Rissa started to open the lid but it sprung open on its own and she was covered in a shower or confetti and polystyrene chips. Everyone burst out laughing. Rissa too was laughing as she lifted out the contents of the box.

'Oh I see,' she said as she removed a large spring from the box. The box also contained a black garter and a cream silk basque with matching knickers.

'Oh, these are really beautiful, thank you everyone,' she said.

'They are to wear on your wedding day,' said Sarah.

'I know my brother will like them,' added Fay, and then looking at her watch she said 'I think its time we moved on to the restaurant.' Rissa folded up her presents and stood up to brush off the confetti, helped by Sarah who picked bits of it out of her hair.

'I'm ready,' said Rissa and they all left the pub to walk the short distance to the restaurant.

Alfredo's had only opened recently and was situated by the river. It already had a reputation for good food, a friendly atmosphere and good-looking waiters. It was these which the girls were talking about as they walked there. They reached the restaurant, entered and were warmly welcomed by Alfredo and Marie, the owner and his wife. Being a Tuesday there were not many diners but Sarah noticed as they were led to their table that there was another large table already laid.

'It looks like they are expecting another large party Rissa,' she said.

'I wonder who,' said Rissa, but she didn't have to wait long to find out - they had only just sat down at the table and were ordering their drinks when the entrance door opened and a crowd of men walked in. They were all well built and smartly dressed in dinner jackets and they were laughing and joking in loud voices as they entered the restaurant. When they saw the table of women they all gave long low wolf whistles and cheered before sitting down at there own table. One of the men came over and spoke to Fay.

'Hello Fay,' he said 'I see you made it then.'

'And you I see have brought the entertainment,' she answered. He laughed and returned to his table.

'That's Ian the vet you work for!' said Rissa. 'Did you set this up?'

'I have to admit to having some hand in it,' admitted Fay grinning. 'Ian was arranging his rugby team's annual outing and I suggested this place as I thought it might liven things up.'

'An excellent idea,' said Simone. 'I propose a toast to Fay,' and they all stood up and drank to Fay. They studied the menus and made their choices and then spent a very enjoyable time flirting with the waiters and exchanging banter with the rugby players throughout the meal. When the meal was finished some of the rugby players wandered over to the table to talk to the girls; they already knew most of them and Anne greeted John, her student from the museum. The waiters came out to move the tables back to make more room for dancing. The first dance was a slow one and Alfredo came out of his kitchen and hurried over to Rissa; he bowed over her hand, kissed it and asked her for a dance. Rissa graciously accepted and the small dapper Italian led her out for the first waltz. When they finished and he led her back to her seat there was loud cheering from the rugby team and Rissa's friends. The other diners looked on smiling but they quickly finished their meals and left the restaurant.

As there was a shortage of women, Rissa and her friends were much in demand for dancing and there was a friendly rivalry between the rugby players and the waiters. Sarah was enjoying herself and she admitted to Rissa when they had a chance to sit down that she hadn't had so much fun in ages.

'It's a far cry from most of the sedate parties that your father and I get invited to nowadays,' she said breathlessly. 'But I am quite exhausted and feeling my age.'

'Your not old, Sarah,' said her stepdaughter; 'Luigi seems quite taken with you.'

'He's probably missing his mother,' replied Sarah.

'Well, he seems to be coming this way again,' said Rissa, and Sarah sighed as she saw the young waiter making his way over to her to ask for another dance. Rissa stayed in her chair and looked around her. She saw that Jenny was again in the arms of John from the museum and Fay had her arms entwined around Ian's neck as they swayed to the music.

'They look cosy together,' she thought. The party continued until midnight when the music stopped and Alfredo came onto the dance floor and clapped his hands.

'It has been a pleasure to have you in our restaurant,' he said. 'I hope that we will see you all again, but before you leave my wife and I would like to offer you some small additional refreshment.' A beaming Marie came through from the kitchen carrying a large cake. She was followed by some of the waiters carrying small glasses and a bottle of grappa. She cut the cake as Alfredo poured everyone a small glass of the pungent liqueur.

'Let us drink to Rissa and wish her every happiness,' he said and everyone toasted Rissa with the grappa and ate a piece of Marie's excellent cake. Alfredo's strong hint that the party was over was taken and everyone prepared to leave the restaurant. Sarah ordered a taxi for Rissa, the Allen girls and herself. The rest of the party were either walking home or sharing taxis. Everyone said goodbye and went their separate ways.

Chapter 31

Fay was in the lavatory at the restaurant preparing to go home. She was pleased that the evening had been such a success but she hoped that for her the night was not yet over. She had had two reasons for suggesting the rugby team went to Alfredo's. The first was to ensure plenty of males for dancing but the second reason was more selfish. She was working at the vets for a year before she went to university and since she had started there last year she had fancied Ian, one of the partners in the practice, and although he seemed to like her he had never asked her out. She had thought tonight she may be able to charm a reaction out of him and it seemed that her plan had worked. She had spent most of the evening in his arms and he had just offered to walk her home. She washed her hands and went to join him.

'It's quite cold tonight,' she said, as she shivered and tucked her arm into Ian's.

'You would have felt warmer if you had thought to wear a coat,' he replied, looking at the flimsy shawl she had wrapped around her shoulders. 'You had better wear mine.' he removed his car coat and wrapped it around her.

'Thanks, but it's a bit big,' said Fay as she put it on. She looked lost in the coat, as although she was tall she was very slim, whereas Ian was over six feet tall with a large muscular frame.

'Never mind, we will soon be home,' he replied.

'But it must a good three miles to my parents,' she said.

'I thought you might like to come to my house for coffee,' he answered. 'It's just round the corner.'

Fay thought that was an excellent idea and arm in arm they walked briskly down the road by the river to Ian's flat. Ian lived on the top two floors of an old converted warehouse and Fay was very impressed when he showed her through the front door. His home consisted of one very large open plan living area with large windows at the end overlooking the river. The room was divided up into a kitchen; dining and seating area and the overall effect was one of light and space. In the corner was a flight of stairs leading to the bedroom and bathroom and the bedroom opened out onto a large balcony.

'You have a great view,' said Fay, walking over to the windows.

'Yes, I was very lucky to buy this when it came on the market. Make yourself comfortable and I will go and brew some coffee.' He left her and went to the kitchen area. Fay walked over to the large sofa, removed his jacket, kicked off her shoes and made herself comfortable lying down on the sofa. Ian brought the coffee over and placed it on a table next to her; he lifted her legs and sat down placing her feet in his lap. He stroked the balls of her feet with his fingers and then lifted her left foot and proceeded to suck her toes one at a time continuing to stroke her other foot and leg with his hand. Fay sighed and he looked over at her and saw that she had her eyes closed but she was smiling. He continued to caress her leg, his hand moving further and further up until he could feel the softness of her silk panties. Fay moaned. Ian stopped what he was doing and stood up. He moved further up the sofa and knelt down on the floor by Fay's head. He lifted up her dress and Fay raised her hips so that he could hitch it up to her waist exposing her long legs and flat stomach. He placed his hand between her legs and stroked her, feeling her wetness through the silk of knickers. He bent down and kissed her on the lips at the same time as slipping a finger inside her knickers to continue stroking her. By now Fay was very wet and Ian could feel himself growing very aroused and straining to escape the confines of his trousers. Fay opened her eyes and lifted herself up into the sitting position; she put her arms behind her neck and undid the button on her halter neck so that when she removed her arms it fell to her waist. She then pushed Ian away and stood up so that her dress fell to the floor and all she was wearing were the black silk knickers. Ian, who was still kneeling took hold of them, pulled them down and pushed his head between her legs licking and sucking on her. Fay didn't want him to stop but she grabbed hold of his hair and pulled him to his feet. She groped for the button on his trousers and with fumbling fingers undid it and pulled his trousers and boxer shorts to his ankles. His member sprang to attention proud and erect and Ian pulled Fay close to him and they kissed passionately while their hands explored each other's bodies. Ian kicked his trousers away and sat down on the sofa pulling Fay on top of him and as she straddled him he entered her. He held her beneath her bottom and as he thrust into her with each stroke he lifted them off the sofa. Fay wrapped her arms around his neck and their lovemaking became more frenzied until Fay was screaming.

'Now, yes now Ian,' and he obliged her by climaxing in one final spurt at the same time as she felt the same exquisite pleasure. They sat there panting until Fay said,

'You never showed me the bedroom, Ian,' and he lifted her up. They collected their clothes and walked up the stairs to his bedroom to spend the rest of the night locked in each other's arms.

Chapter 32

Before Kathryn returned from Chadsbury Hall, Lady Viola had carried out the rest of her plan. She spoke to her son about appointing William Aleyn as the next bailiff. Thomas told her that Roger Tyler had already spoken to him about retiring and he had recommended Aleyn as his successor. Thomas had made the decision to appoint William Aleyn as the new bailiff and intended to speak to him soon. Viola asked Thomas to delay the announcement until Kathryn had returned home and until she thought that the time was right. He agreed, never thinking to ask his mother why. He knew she must have her reasons.

Viola summoned William Aleyn, from the village and she was waiting for him in the solar when he arrived.

'Good day, Lady Viola,' he said to her confidently. 'I take it you have considered my proposition. I understand that Lady Kathryn is with child.' His meaning was clear.

Viola intended to be in charge of this meeting and she said in her most icy tone.

'That doesn't concern you, William. I have thought about what we talked about and I would like you to do something for me. If you carry out this task effectively I will guarantee that you will be the next bailiff'.

'What is it you want me to do?' asked William, realising his life long ambition was nearly in reach.

'What I am to ask of you is between you and me and must never be spoken of again, is that clear?' she said.

'Agreed.'

'I want you to ensure that Brother Francis disappears from this area never to return. I do not want him to be able to contact anyone here ever again. I want him gone before Lady Kathryn returns from Kilborough. If you can do this for me then I promise that you will be our new bailiff.'

William looked at Viola with admiration on his face; he understood exactly what she meant and he said,

'You want me to make sure he is never seen again?'

'I think you understand me,' she replied curtly. 'The day following his disappearance you will be bailiff.' And at this she turned away from him.

William guessed that he was dismissed and left the room.

Viola breathed a sigh of relief and hoped he could carry out her wishes soon.

On their return from Kilborough Francis told his uncle of his decision to return to his monastery. His uncle was disappointed and tried to persuade him otherwise.

'I have my reasons uncle; Chadsbury Green is

not the place where my future lies. I shall go before the end of September, that will give me time to hand over the school to Lady Margaret and tie up any other loose ends.'

Henry Wodewarde was a wise man and he too had noticed the blossoming friendship between his nephew and Kathryn and he guessed that Francis wanted to leave before she returned, but he kept his own counsel.

'If you are sure that is what you want then I will not stand in your way. I shall sorely miss your company and I hope you will have time to write to me.'

'I shall certainly write to you uncle, and you must write to me and let me know all the gossip from the village and the progress of the new de Montagu heir.' Francis said.

Francis made his preparations for his departure. He spoke to Margaret and she promised to take care of his school.

'My uncle will be writing to me Lady Margaret, I would be grateful if you could spare the time to write to me occasionally and report on the children's learning. My uncle could forward your letters to me,' he asked. She readily agreed.

When it was near the time for him to leave, Francis went and said goodbye to all the villagers that he had got to know and grown fond of. He also called on Sir Thomas de Montagu.

'Kathryn will be sorry not to have been here to

say goodbye,' said Thomas.

'Perhaps you will say goodbye for me Sir Thomas,' said Francis. 'I would like to leave you with a book of French poetry that I would like Kathryn to have.'

'That is very kind of you,' said Thomas taking the book from Francis. 'I shall make sure she gets it. I am very grateful for all you have done this summer. You know you will always be welcome here if you ever return to this part of the world.'

'It was my pleasure,' said Francis, feeling guilty.

William Aleyn had thought for a long time about the meaning behind Viola's words. He had heard that Francis was leaving the village but he knew that that was not what she wanted. The night before Francis was intending to leave he called to his son and said that he wanted to speak to him. William took him to the churchyard and on the way there he spoke to him.

'You're a bright lad, Robert and I have something that I want you to help me with. I intend to be the bailiff at Chadsbury Hall and I want you to follow in my footsteps.'

'I hope you can be father, Molly would be so proud if she knew I was to be the bailiff,' replied Robert eagerly.

'But before I can have the job there is something I must do and you have to help me. You must promise me that you never tell anyone what we do tonight, not even Molly.'

'Anything you say father, you know that,' said Robert.

'You are a good boy,' said his father and proceeded to tell him what they had to do. Roberts's eyes widened in horror and he gulped.

'Is this necessary?' he asked.

'Believe me it is, and I know I can rely on you.' continued William. 'I will wait in the churchyard and I want you to go and find Brother Francis and give him a message. Tell him that Lady Margaret would like to speak to him now before he leaves and that she is waiting in the church. When you return I shall be waiting for him.'

Robert was scared but he did not ask anymore questions - he knew better than to argue with his father.

'I had better go then,' he said and loped off into the night.

When he had gone William looked around the churchyard for a suitable hiding place. It was a cold night with no moon. A damp white fog hung over the graves; an ideal night thought William. He chose to hide behind a large grave marker close to the side wall of the church. He crouched down and waited.

Robert had found Francis and given him his father's message; he was nervous but Francis had not noticed and said that he would come straight-away.

'I hope Robert you will continue with your lessons with Lady Margaret once I am gone,' said Francis.

'Yes Sir,' said Robert, trying to sound normal. 'It's cold tonight.'

'It will be even colder where I am going,' answered Francis. Robert did not know how to answer that and did not reply. Francis attempted to have a further conversation with Robert but all he got were monosyllabic answers so he gave up and they continued without speaking. When they reached the church Francis turned to Robert and told him to go home but before he had finished speaking William leapt from his hiding place and struck Francis on the back of the head with a large jagged stone. Francis fell to the ground.

'Quickly Robert, hold him for me before he comes round,' said William whispering.

Shaking with terror Robert did as he was bid he straddled Francis and pinioned his arms to the sides of his body. Francis opened his eyes groaning as he did so but before he had a chance to struggle William had removed a knife from his clothing and stabbed Francis. The knife went under his ribs and into his heart. He died instantly.

Chapter 33

Rissa awoke on Wednesday morning with a pounding headache. She had a long shower, dressed in her riding clothes and walked gingerly down the stairs and into breakfast. Luckily her brother and sister had left for school, her father was already in his office and there was only Sarah seated at the table.

'Good Morning Sarah,' she whispered.

'Oh dear, you look as bad as I feel,' said Sarah. 'I think I had a bit too much to drink last night and I ache all over from dancing. There's a fresh pot of coffee on the sideboard you look like you need it.'

'That and a large glass of orange juice will do me this morning,' groaned Rissa. 'Still it was worth it, I'm glad everyone had a good time.' The door opened and Tom walked in.

'I see you've made it down at last,' he said.

'Don't shout daddy,' said Rissa softly.

'I see you are a little worse for wear like Sarah. It seems I missed out on all the fun. I just came in to say that I have had Sergeant Bridges on the phone; they are asking everyone in the neighbourhood to look for any signs of Richard. They are hoping to find his car, as so far there has been no sign of it at the ports or airports and no one has reported it abandoned in a car park. He asked me if I could arrange a search of our land and I agreed. Any volunteers?'

'A walk in the fresh air would probably help my head,' said Sarah. 'I could take a stroll around our grounds but I think we may have noticed if Richard was lurking in the bushes.'

'But at least we can say we tried,' said her husband. 'And what about you Rissa?'

'I thought a good long ride would clear my head, so there is no reason for me not to look for Richards's car at the same time. Where would you like me to go?'

'Drop into the office when you're ready and we will look at the map,' said Tom. Rissa and Sarah finished their breakfast in silence and cleared the table.

'I'll see you later,' said Rissa and she went to join her father in his office.

'Oh there you are Rissa,' he said, studying the estate map. 'I have circled an area for you to search near the stables. I thought you could take the track up to the old quarry and circle back through the woods. Is that OK?'

'Fine by me,' she answered.

'You had better take your mobile in case you find anything,' Tom said.

'I doubt I will,' replied Rissa, going up to her room to get ready. When she came back down the stairs she went out to the car and whistled for the dogs, Boris and Teddy, who came bounding to her from round the side of the house followed by her father.

'I thought I would take them with me,' she said

'In that case you had better take the Land Rover,' he said, and gave her the keys. She walked over to it and opened it up and the dogs leapt in. She put it into gear and waved to her father as she drove down the drive to the stables.

At the stables she saw a very fragile looking Jenny sitting outside one of the loose-boxes, cleaning a bridle.

'You managed to get to work then?' asked Rissa.

'Yes, but as you can see I am not rushing around - I feel a little delicate this morning!'

'Me too, I am going for a ride to clear my head. Dad has asked me to look out for signs of Richard, the police have asked him to search the estate.'

'Yes I know, your father telephoned earlier and asked us to look in all the loose-boxes and outbuildings. As if we wouldn't have noticed a strange car hiding in the stables.'

'I know what you mean but dad is taking it very seriously. Changing the subject I see you were having a good time last night, why is it that all of a sudden the Allen family are attracted to archaeologists?'

'Oh you mean John,' she replied a slow blush creeping up her neck. 'I like him, he wants to see me again and I have arranged to meet him on Thursday night in the Angel.'

'I'm glad you had a good time, I'll go and saddle

Dreamer and leave you to your cleaning. Rissa went to find her horse and put his saddle and bridle on; she fetched the dogs from the Land Rover, mounted Dreamer and set off towards the track to the quarry. It started to drizzle and by the time she reached the quarry the rain was pouring down and they were all getting very wet.

The quarry had been in use for a number of years and through the rain looked a very desolate place. The old shed that the workmen had used in the days when the quarry was in full use was still in good repair and occasionally used by the estate workers to store equipment. Rissa knew where the key was kept and thought she would take the animals in there to shelter until the rain eased off. She guided Dreamer carefully around the lake, which had formed at the bottom of the quarry, and they made their way to the shed. When they reached it she dismounted, tethered her horse and went to find the key. The key was in its usual hiding place under a stone at the side of the shed and Rissa took it and went to open the large doors. She pulled them open and went to fetch Dreamer. Boris and Teddy had already entered when she opened the door. As she led the horse in she realised that there was a car inside and the dogs were growling - she recognised it as Richard's car!

Rissa felt her heart beating faster and she found that she was shaking. She tied the horse up near the door and tentatively approached the car - it was empty. She gave a sigh of relief and tried the car door and found it unlocked. She opened it and looked inside. The keys were still in the ignition and on the seat were a wallet and a letter. She reached in to remove them and then remembered that she ought to leave them for the police to find. With shaking hands she reached into her pocket to call her father on her mobile 'phone but found that she was unable to get a signal. She shut the car door and went out into the rain to see if she could get a better signal outside. There was an improvement and she pressed in the numbers for her father's mobile.

When he answered she said,

'Dad, I have found Richard's car at the quarry,' she didn't hear his reply as the mobile signal was very faint and so she left her mobile on and went to shelter from the rain hoping someone would come quickly.

While she was on the phone Boris and Teddy had raced out of the shed and were now barking furiously. She stood up and went to look outside and saw them down by the lake barking at an object in the water. She left the shelter of the barn and walked down to the water to join them. They were standing at the waters edge standing over something. She moved closer and saw that they had found Richard!

Rissa stood there for a long time looking at the

body in the water. She felt nauseous and turned to run back to the safety of the shed, when she bent over and was violently sick. She went in to the shed and sat on the floor by the horse shaking. The dogs came to join her and she held them close to her as she sat and watched the rain pouring down outside. It seemed like she had been sitting there for ages when she heard the noise of a car. She raced out of the shed and saw several police cars coming down the track to the quarry. Leading the police cars was her father in the Land Rover. She ran over to him and when he got out of the car she flung herself into his arms crying.

'It's all right Rissa,' he said gently. 'We came as quickly as we could - you said that you have found Richard's car in the shed?'

Rissa managed to speak and said.

'There's a body in the water, I think its Richard.'

Tom called the police over and told them what she had said.

'Do you think you can show me where Rissa?' said Roger Lacy, the chief inspector. Tom released his hold on Rissa and took her hand, and she took them down to the waters edge and pointed to where the body lay.

'His car is in the shed, there is a wallet and letter on the front seat but I didn't touch anything,' she said.

Lacy shouted some orders to his men and he

went with Rissa and Tom to the barn. Dreamer was very restless and nervous because of all the strangers and Rissa went over to him to try and calm him down. The chief inspector put on a pair of surgical gloves, opened the car door and carefully removed the wallet and letter. He opened the wallet and checked its contents and then looked at the letter, he frowned and walked over to Rissa and her father.

'The wallet belongs to Richard Harvey and the letter is addressed to Sarah. I believe that is your wife's name Sir?' he said to Tom.

'Yes,' said Tom.

'Well Sir, under the circumstances I think we had better open it, I take it you or you wife would have no objection?'

'No, go ahead,' replied Tom, gripping his daughter's hand tightly. 'We have nothing to hide.'

Roger Lacy slit open the envelope, removed the letter and read it. When he had finished he said,

'I think this explains everything; would you like to hear what he has written?'

'It would be best,' said Tom.

'My dear Sarah, I spoke to your husband this afternoon and we had a terrible argument. After he left I realised that my love for you was futile. I was foolish to believe that I could persuade you to run away with me. I know now that you truly love your husband, he is a good man and I know that he loves you as much as you love him and that he will always take great care of you. Without your love I am unable to carry on in this world and so I have decided to take my own life and pass in to the next world where I might find true happiness. I hope you will remember me with some affection. Yours ever, Richard.'

Chapter 34

The sun was shining when Rissa opened the curtains on Saturday morning. There was a knock on her door and Sarah entered the room carrying a tray.

'I've brought you your breakfast, the bride needs to be pampered on her wedding day,' said Sarah.

'What a lovely thought,' said Rissa and kissed Sarah. 'I was just thinking how strange it will be to live somewhere else, I have only ever lived here and I am going to miss all of you very much.'

'You're hardly moving far,' Sarah said laughing.

'Even so I am feeling sad. I know the bride is supposed to be happy but I keep thinking of Richard and also the pilgrim who met such tragic ends.'

'You mustn't, there is no time; we still have plenty to do this morning before you go to the church,' said Sarah lightly. They both heard footsteps running up the stairs and Harry and Lucy raced into the room.

'Slow down you two,' their mother said sternly.

'We wanted to give Rissa our present,' said Lucy excitedly.

'Perhaps you should wait for your father,' said Sarah. 'Here he is now,' and Tom appeared at the door beaming.

'How is my little girl,' he said. 'Already for her

big day'.

'I feel fine but I think my quiet breakfast has just gone by the board,' answered Rissa.

'Well, I wanted you to have this and as these two couldn't wait I thought I had better join them,' and he handed her a jewellery case. Rissa opened it and looked at the gold, sapphire and pearl necklace nestling inside the case.

'It's beautiful, dad.'

'It was your mothers; I know she would have wanted you to wear it today,' he said gruffly.

'This is from us,' said Harry, and he thrust a gaily wrapped parcel into her hands. She opened it and inside was a small enamel and silver box.

'You can put it on your dressing table so that you don't forget us,' said Lucy.

'I shall always treasure it,' said Rissa.

'I too have something for you,' said Sarah. 'I didn't want to feel left out.' She gave Rissa another small box that contained some sapphire and pearl earrings. 'When Tom said he was giving you your mother's necklace I went out to find some earrings to match it.'

'Thank you all so much,' said Rissa and she hugged and kissed everyone in turn, crying as she did so.

'Out you two, let Rissa have some peace,' said Sarah and she took her two children and pushed them out of the door in front of her.

Tom was left alone with his daughter and he turned to her and said,

'Your mother would have been so proud of you. I am sorry she is not able to see you now.'

'I know dad, but I don't really remember her and I will have you and Sarah. Sarah has been a very good mother to me, I was very lucky that you found her.'

'I agree she's a marvellous woman and she makes me very happy,' he said.

The rest of the morning sped quickly by. Fay arrived mid morning to get changed and to assist Rissa. Sarah, Harry and Mrs White left for the church and then so did the two bridesmaids. Rissa dressed in her wedding gown and donned her mother's necklace, and then walked down the stairs to where her father was waiting. As he helped her into the limousine he had tears in his eyes as he whispered

'You look just like your mother.'

The car drove off, and Rissa turned to look at Chadsbury Hall as she left it for the last time before starting her new life as Simon's wife.

It was a cold night in early February. It had been snowing since early that morning and the ground outside Chadsbury Hall was covered with a thick blanket of white. Inside the Hall Thomas de Montagu sat in his room, the wind was howling and he had drunk a flagon of wine and had started on his second but he could still hear the sounds of his wife's screams coming from upstairs.

Kathryn had gone into labour earlier that day. Jane Smithson was in attendance and helping her were Margaret, Viola and Mary Leys. It had been a long labour and the room was hot and stuffy.

'We are nearly there my lady, I can see the baby's head,' said Jane. 'If you can manage one extra hard push next time I think we will do it.'

Kathryn nodded her head weakly and her mother mopped the sweat from her brow.

'It won't be much longer my love,' said her mother.

'Keep pushing,' shouted Jane. 'It's coming.' Kathryn gave one long last push and felt the relief as the baby was born. Jane cut the cord and turned the child upside down and he started to cry. Viola took him from Jane and wrapped him in a shawl and placed him in Kathryn's arms.

'It's a boy,' she said to Kathryn. 'You have a son!'

Kathryn looked down at the small bundle in her arms and smiled weakly.

'I shall call him Francis,' she said.